I Remain

Megan Hutton

Brainspired Publishing

Ontario, Canada

I Remain

Copyright © 2023 2nd Edition
1st Editions: Alpha - June 2023, Beta - September 2023
Megan Hutton All rights reserved.
Cover design by *Davina Hader* **Studio Conceptions**, Toronto, Ontario, Canada

The author of this work has portrayed real-life events in a truthful manner based on their recollection and research. Dialogue has been added to accurately represent the character or nature of the speaker. All individuals mentioned are real, and there are no fictional characters. To respect the privacy of some individuals, some names may have been changed.

Visit my website at www.meganhutton.ca
Visit my author page at https://brainspiredpublishing.com/megan-hutton

Brainspired Publishing
A joint venture of Brainchild Holdings Inc. and INspired Media Inc.
Ontario, Canada

www.brainspiredpublishing.com

PAPERBACK ISBN: 9781-7387469-2-8
Library and Archives Canada / Government of Canada Tel: 819-953-3997 or 1-866-578-7777

Acknowledgements

I wrote this memoir to give my mother's life meaning, as well as my own. As a child, I experienced a system designed to keep vulnerable and powerless women with few choices.

A patriarchal society drove her to an ill-fated union, and her future children would also suffer. She was more than an overwhelmed mother to her twelve children. Before she was judged by society as a single mother, she was in love. My mother foresaw a different future than the one she would live.

This was evidenced in our numerous conversations and the letters she wrote to the man she was in love with for years. I was a child who observed her from a young age and I could feel the longing and sadness she carried. I lived in a house of secrets. At the age of five, I knew that my father's angry words aimed at my mother had something to do with me, "I'm going to tell her what you did." It would be decades before I understood his words.

Eventually, my mother's sadness turned into resignation. I vowed mine would be different. I played with dolls, but they never had a father figure. I rejected the idea of marriage at first but desperately wanted children. Looking back, I wanted to recreate my own childhood and do it differently for my own children. I didn't date and was often referred to as a lesbian. All came to pass; I had my children and came out as a lesbian in my thirties. I escaped from my home at fourteen and set off on my own path, alone in the world. I could finally stop holding my breath, and live my life void of constant unpredictability, and violence.

Jane Walsh was the first therapist who helped me unlock doors. She led me to a place of healing, and I finally understood there was nothing wrong with me. My early tenacity and positive outlook made me a survivor, although my body memory stays with me. Later in life, after I was able to acknowledge the lack of attachments throughout my life, Colleen Hood and I delved deeper into the affects of trauma and grief and the feelings of loss that I carried with me. Molly Peacock has been instrumental in me believing in my work. She is a gifted writer, and unbelievably generous with her time. Molly is one of those gifts in a lifetime. Molly's encouragement and belief in my work changed my life.

Bronwyn Drainie, journalist, author and editor, was a brilliant and insightful editor. I felt validated when she took on my memoir and trusted her with my story. Max Wallace has too many accolades to mention, a New York Times bestseller and extraordinary human being who took time to read my work and offer valuable insights. We met accidentally at a Joan Baez concert, our love of folk music and writing apparent after a brief conversation.

Poet Kate Marshall Flaherty is part of an ongoing group of five women writers I'm part of. We're going into our 6th year, confiding and supporting one another, each on our own personal journeys. Kate is a talented poet, a wonderful confident, and encouraging friend.

My memories of a long-ago friendship with Eric Wilson, from my latter teens have also been a catalyst for me. Eric sold over a million books with his children's series Tom and Liz Austen. It was a pleasure to write about the time we spent together at the beginning of our adult lives. My dear friend Judith McCaffery is a wonderful soul sister, providing a critique when I needed it and encouragement when I was overwhelmed with memories. I'm humbled to have the support of these talented writers. Much gratitude to Davina Hader, your love and friendship over the past decade means so much to me. Love and gratitude to my partner Autumn, and my granddaughter Madison for spending hours deciphering my longhand and typing it into the computer when I was too exhausted. To my adult children, Jamie and Mandy, thank you for allowing me to share our story. I wish we could do a redo of your childhood with the wisdom I have now. For the next generation, Madison, Noah, Morgan, Sebastian, Olivia, Wyatt, Ireland, Avery and Vance...children have a way of helping us to heal. Love and gratitude to Elaine Adams for gifting me with my mother's original letters to her father. Thank you to my numerous Beta readers who gave me feedback and encouragement. Thank you in particular to my aunt Helen, my mom's 92 year old sister who read my draft and was saddened by the revelations about my mom's life. Thank you to my mom's other surviving sister, Alberteen who is 94. Her comment to me was, " I don't understand why she didn't leave that miserable bastard."

Finally, to all my siblings. You will have your own memories and versions of your early lives. This is my story from my personal observations and memories. In addition, I accessed dozens of my mother's letters, and the hours of videos where she shared long held secrets about her past.

I hope you can hear her voice in my words and remember how much we all meant to her.

CONTENTS

If I Die

Now I lay me.

If I die

A small child
prays.

The fear of sleeping
and being awake

Now I lay me
hands clasped.

Small fingers
entwined.

If I die
before I wake

Prologue

While John's baby grew inside her, Syl denied its existence, right up until her fifth month. She would learn later that every new life has a reason and, in some cases, a tenacity that refuses to let go. Lying between the folds of what could have been and what was, is the truth. For an unborn baby, it could be a story about love and passion, or a story about regret. In the far reaches of what would exist, I could only imagine what my mother's thoughts and feelings were during this time.

Syl, for her part, decided to document these few months before her pregnancy was terminated. She had a child inside her and could only imagine what it would say.

Dear Fetus:

If anyone knew I was writing to you they would put me away. It may be selfish of me to want a connection, but I know that I am making the right decision given my circumstances. If I were to keep you, I would be tied to a man I don't love. Life is full of regrets this will be one of them.

Dear Mama:

Regrets? There are soft sounds. I can feel your body when it moves.

Dear Fetus:

Today I used a wire hanger to try to dislodge you. It's upsetting to know that I'm trying to end a life that has barely begun. I'm fighting my own personal war. Our lives don't always work out as planned. If the hanger reached you, I am sorry. I hope I didn't cause you any pain. I did some damage to myself, but that will heal.

Dear Mama:

Pain? I am still here. The hanger did not reach me. In my own way, I suppose I am grateful. I'm not sure what all of this means but it sounds like a humble way to say thank you for another day. Don't be sorry. If this is all I ever know, I won't know any different.

Dear Fetus:

I know that you are about three inches long now, and all your organs are in place. You have tiny fingernails. I have always dreamed of having a little girl. If you were a girl and I were to keep you, I would have painted them pink to match your first birthday dress.

Dear Mama:

Pink? Birthday? Pain?

Dear Fetus:

Pain is easy to explain. It can be caused by events or people outside of ourselves. We can also manifest it with our own thoughts. Pain can be physical or emotional. I'm experiencing both. Something called love lies between pain and loss.

Dear Mama:

When you put your hands on your belly, does that mean you love me?

Dear Fetus:

You are proving to be much stronger than I anticipated. I am sorry if you are suffering from the toxic liquids I took last night. I'm not faring well either and was violently ill last night. Once again, there is no indication that you have let go. In my own way I love it that you are so tenacious. I wish I was able to meet you, but I know that isn't possible. There will be an emptiness inside me when you are gone. Love is a complicated feeling.

Dear Mama:

I felt your body tremble last night and I became very still, but I am here. Tell me about love again. I hope one day I can feel it. Have you changed your mind? I haven't felt anything different for a few days.

Dear Fetus:

The love I feel for you has no boundaries because we will never meet. It will be our secret. We will be connected in a time that will remain infinite. Explaining love is as difficult as attempting to explain life. It often defies reason and sensibility. Love can lead us to unpredictable and foolish actions. Love is not a sure thing. Pain and love often go hand in hand. Where there is gain eventually there will be a loss. The state of being in love can often override rational thought. We survive love, lost or found. Letting go of expectations takes a long time to learn. You and I both need to let go.

Dear Mama:

There are so many mysteries about love I will never know. I wish you would love me enough to let me live.

Dear Fetus:

I don't want to write about love anymore. It doesn't seem right when I'm filled with sadness. When I watch my little boy play, he looks so happy. I think about who you might have been. When he tucks his small hand into mine or touches my cheek, I wonder what it would be like to feel yours. My body appears to want you to stay intact. You've proven to be difficult to expel. My mind is in a different place. This is the duality of love. If you were to have a life outside my body, you would see the sun. We need sun to survive. We can't always see it. The sun goes up and down, just like love and being happy. In many ways you are fortunate. You will never know love, loss, happy or sad.

Dear Mama:

Today my fingers touched. Now I know that I am real.

Dear Fetus:

You are about five inches long now. I am so sorry. Tomorrow I am going to make another attempt. Please let go, this isn't pleasant for either of us. It's evident that we are at an impasse. That is what happens when two opposing forces want different outcomes. Not a day will go by that I don't wonder who you might have been.

Dear Mama:

Today my fingers touched my toes and then my eye. I will wait for tomorrow and hope for more tomorrows after that. I love you. I am not going away.

All of life's secrets are not available for our scrutiny. What if the wire coat hanger had reached into my mother's soft folds far enough to snuff out the beginning of a new life that was me? What if hanging onto my only life source was taken away before I could see the light of day? Becoming aware of the circumstances of my tenuous survival, later in life I erased it from my body memory.

Body memory survives crude wire coat hangers and toxic fluids. It dissolves into questions we can't answer and questions there are no need to ask. The journey that becomes our life is the only answer.

A struggling embryo has no voice. A fetus with a brain, limbs and finely formed fingers that can intertwine cannot call out. Those tiny fingernails my mother painted pink to match my first birthday dress is her memory. My body memory is mine alone.

Somewhere within all of us lies experiences with no voice, no way to call out. We cling to trust before we are born into this world, trust we will survive. In our outer world we cling to trust and the promise that all will be possible.

Life is about hanging on while threads of who we were, and threads of who we have become merge, and once again, the journey becomes the answer.

I Remain

Syl held her hands over her belly as the Canadian National's wheels sparked and screeched slowly forward. The train was the lifeblood of this isolated Northern B.C. Community; its mournful whistle had marked the passing of time, births, and deaths. It was the lullaby of Syl's childhood, and it seemed only fitting the train would carry her off to begin a life of her own. The week before, the same train had taken the love of her short life, Hugh, to war. The child she knew was growing inside her remained a secret.

Now Syl was leaving all she had known and traveling to Vancouver to give birth and secure a job at the shipyards. A home for unwed mothers – Baywood - was her first destination. A friend had told her that this would be a safe place until she gave birth. Syl marked the passing of time watching the telephone poles until the train gained momentum, and the poles became one long line, lulling her into a deep slumber. She awoke abruptly when the train whistle signaled, they reached their destination.

"Don't forget your bag miss."

The conductor wondered why a young woman like Syl was out alone in the city. Her looks and diminutive size belied her twenty-plus years. Syl gathered her one small bag and coat. The trolley she needed to get to the home was a short walk from the train station. Soon, she'd be somewhere warm and safe, at least for the time being. The trolley dropped her off across from a large white house, at least three storeys high, with an inviting sign on the front lawn.

"Baywood: All Women Welcome, a Place of Safety."

Syl's experience with strangers was limited. There was a moment of doubt and hesitation before she lifted the brass knocker and announced her presence. The door sprang open; a buxom woman stood firmly in the entrance.

"And who might you be?"

She greeted Syl and nodded for her to step inside. She noticed Syl's hands clasped protectively over her belly.

"It looks like you're in the right place, somehow they all find us, I'm Effie, I run the office, let's take down some information and get you settled."

Effie was an imposing figure. She wore a large black bonnet tied at the side, with an equally large black ribbon. There was a sign over her desk that read:

"The Salvation Army Saves Sinners."

Effie puffed up her ample bosom, as though she was going to give glory to God at that very moment. Syl wanted to make it clear from the onset that she didn't consider herself a sinner.

"My fiancé was called to serve overseas, and we…"

Effie looked over her shoulder at a large picture of Jesus. He was wearing a crown of thrones, blood dripping from his hands and feet.

"Now, now, we are all sinners, no one is exempt."

Syl didn't feel as safe as she had a few moments before. Something told her to keep her thoughts to herself. Effie took down some information, rang a bell, and another woman in a large bonnet appeared.

"Maria will take you to your room, be with God, Syl."

Syl was led up a flight of stairs to a large dorm style room with six beds.

"Take your clothes off and put them in this bag."

Maria left the room while Syl undressed. Syl had sewn the small amount of money her brother Wallace had given her into the lining of her coat. She pulled it out, folded it quickly and stuck it under her mattress. Maria returned and took Syl's bag of clothes.

"Our assurance that you won't run off."

Syl was now almost certain this wasn't a safe place, but she was new to the city and had nowhere else to go. She decided to keep her eyes and ears open, and her mouth closed. Almost as soon as she arrived, she began to plan her escape. The hypocrisy and cracks appeared quickly. The pious attitudes of Effie and Maria were anything but God-like. Syl watched young girls disappear onto the upper floors as their due dates approached. She never saw them again, or their babies. One night, a young girl about fifteen, was crying softly in her bed. Although Syl tried to keep to herself, she went over to see if she could comfort her. The girl threw her skinny arms around Syl's neck.

"Can you help me? I want to talk to my mother, and they won't let me."

The girl was frantic and trembling, but Syl didn't want to give her false hope.

"I'll do what I can, but we are all in the same boat."

Syl was thankful for the money her brother had given her. He was sworn to secrecy about the pregnancy, and although she was about seven months along, her belly barely showed. She knew the birth time was not far away and she needed a plan. Effie and Maria had already noted that Syl was no trouble. She was the first to offer a hand, and because she had earned their trust, she was given some leniency. There was no indication that Syl had carefully plotted her escape.

A month later, Syl was summoned to the office. Effie sensed they were dealing with a strong young woman who had a mind of her own. Syl sensed she needed to tread with caution.

"We've been discussing your situation, and we think the best option is to give your child up for adoption."

Syl remained silent. Effie folded her hands across her bosom and continued.

"We think every child deserves a good home with two parents from the beginning."

Syl suspected this was coming. She had planned accordingly. Syl nodded in compliance, as was her habit with Effie.

"Just give me a couple of days to let this sink in."

Effie nodded, watching Syl walk slowly back up the stairs to her room.

"That was easy."

Effie smiled at Maria, who nodded like the good second fiddle she had become.

"She won't miss one, I'm sure there will be more babies in her future."

The following week, Syl knew that the time to leave had arrived. She'd become friendly with Fiona, a young woman who stayed on at the home as a night worker after the birth of her child. Syl listened for the clickity clack, of heavy black oxfords, as Fiona came up the stairs to do the night checks.

"Fiona, I'm feeling a bit queasy tonight, do you mind if I go down to the kitchen for some warm milk?"

Fiona glanced at the door. She knew that Effie and Maria would be in their rooms on the third floor by now.

"Wait until I'm done, then creep down the back stairs, and be quick."

As soon as Fiona left the room, Syl rolled her nightgown up around her bulging stomach and put her coat on. She took the money out from under her mattress and stuck it in her coat pocket. She made her way down to the kitchen. Being compliant had paid off. She knew that the back door in the kitchen led to the alley, and quietly made her exit. She walked quickly down the street, catching sight of a trolley stop about a block away. She boarded, moving towards the centre of the city. Soon she was far away from the safe home that felt like a prison. Syl had no idea where she was going. She waited until she spotted a rooming house with a porch light on and noticed the trolley driver looking at her with suspicion.

"What's a young woman in your condition doing out on your own at this time of night?"

Syl moved towards the door not answering him.

"This is my stop. Thank you and goodnight."

She watched him shake his head as she began to cross the deserted street. Under the porch light there was a sign, 'Women's Rooming House, Long Term Only Need Apply.'

Under that unspoken warning - ladies of the night not wanted here - was the owner's name and room number.

'Owner, Gladys, Ring Suite Six. Open from 6:00 A.M until midnight.'

It was a quarter to 12:00 when Syl pushed the small black buzzer. A pleasant-looking middle-aged women opened the door. Syl was relieved.

"I'm looking for a room, you see, I'm…"

"Yes, I can see that,"

Gladys ushered her in, locking the front door.

"I have one small room I can give you for now."

Gladys took Syl to her own small owner's suite first. It reminded Syl of her mother's kitchen. The landlady was about her mother's age. That alone gave her comfort.

"Let's get a hot cup of tea in you, and then I'll show you to your room."

Gladys too, was relieved.

"This time of night, the rings are usually from young women out looking for trouble, or too drunk to go home."

"I'll pay for my room tomorrow. I have money put away until I get a job."

Gladys put the kettle on the cook stove, patiently waiting for the whistle.

"No need to worry about money just yet, we'll work something out. I could use help in the office."

Syl was relieved she stopped here, grateful for an accepting host. She explained her situation and Gladys just took it all in quietly.

"He did offer me a place to wait for the birth of our baby, at his sister's, but I didn't want to go."

It was as though Syl wasn't sure anymore. What did Hugh think about having a baby with her? Time would tell. Syl woke up early the next morning. She was looking out at a woman with flaming red curls, across the street, turning a window sign from, 'CLOSED,' to, 'OPEN.' The larger sign on top of the building read, 'The True Love Cafe.'

Gladys knocked quietly on Syl's door.

"You're awake already,"

Syl already had a comfort level with Gladys.

"I forgot where I was, I'm used to an early rise, my grandmother used to say, "Use your hours wisely, you're dead long enough.""

Gladys and Syl both laughed.

"I see that Vi has her,' OPEN' sign out," Gladys commented.

Syl pulled the curtain wide open.

"Yes, and I can see people going in already."

Gladys came back to the window.

"Vi is the salt of the earth, she's made her cafe like a second home for everyone around here."

Syl felt certain that something had to go wrong. Her new life, even on day one, felt almost perfect.

"Do you mind if I smoke in here?"

Syl's habit had grabbed her by the throat by the time she turned eleven.

"Just don't burn the place down,"

Gladys laughed.

"I'll grab you an ashtray from the office, I quit five years ago."

Soon Syl and Gladys were swapping stories as if they'd been friends for years.

"This baby, what's your plan?"

Gladys and Syl had walked down the dimly lit hall to Gladys's own apartment.

"Well, it has to come out, that part I know for sure."

Syl took a slow sip from her coffee mug.

"I'll start looking for work tomorrow, hopefully night shifts, so I can get someone to stay with the baby."

Gladys now stood by her own window, deep in thought.

"You came along at the right time Syl. Apart from this rooming house, my life has been lonely. I always wanted a child, but it wasn't in the cards for me." She turned and walked over to Syl.

"We'll work this out together, I'll help wherever I can."

Syl was speechless. In one day, she'd gone from a place where her baby was going to be taken from her, to an embracing home. That night she settled into what would be a new comfort, sure she was in the right place. The following week she wrote to Hugh.

Dear Hugh: January 2, 1944.

I hope you received the socks and candy I sent you for Christ-mas. With all the rations it's not always easy to get what I want. Gladys is an angel. I help in the office and landed a part time job as a riveter at the shipyards. It keeps my mind off wishing you were here. Our baby is due next month. I'll be leaving the shipyards at the end of this week. I don't mind the work but sometimes it's dangerous. Last week a red-hot rivet just missed my eye. On Friday, a dolly bar slammed onto my foot, it took the top right off my little toe. The good thing is, I know I have a job to come back to after the baby comes. Just remember that I love you. I am waiting for you. The next time I write, we will be parents.

All my love and kisses, Syl.

Syl's resilience was an asset. In her short life she had dealt with more than most. Years earlier, the family had lost Syl's nine-year-old brother in the Fraser River. She looked at life as a progression of events, thinking they would unfold in an order dictated by a force much larger than herself. On a frigid February morning, she awoke to find her bed soaked. She lit a cigarette, and walked down the hall to get Gladys.

"I think the baby is on the way."

She was calm as she made her way into Gladys's suite. The second bedroom was all prepared, a clean sheet on the bed, everything they would need close at hand.

"Geez Syl, do you need to smoke now?"

Syl reluctantly put it out and climbed onto the bed.

"Let's get this baby out."

Gladys was usually calm, but now looking a bit frazzled. Syl, on the other hand, witnessed numerous births of her younger siblings, all at home. She knew that nature would eventually take its course. A healthy baby boy pushed his presence into a blustery February evening. Syl and Gladys drank tea, then watched him sleep.

Syl's job at the shipyards was waiting just as Jake the foreman had promised. He was surprised to see her so soon, a week after giving birth.

"No rest for the wicked, eh, Syl."

He could be a pain in the ass, but Syl knew he had a good heart.

It was a hell of a lot more fun getting it in there than having it come out."

Jake laughed and they wound their way through the large warship to Syl's station.

"Back to work."

She was hoping to find a letter waiting when she arrived home. She'd written to Hugh and shared the news that he had a son.

Dear Hugh: February 28, 1944:

Our son just missed being born as a leap year baby by a few hours. He already has signs that he has your blond curls. He is a strapping baby, weighing in at eight pounds! As soon as I'm able I'll get a picture to you daddy! How does it feel? I'm looking forward to the day when we are all together. Stay safe, we need you to come home.

Forever yours, xox

Syl sealed the envelope with her lipstick kisses. No reply from Hugh came when she returned from her first day back at the shipyard. Syl worked the evening shift while Gladys took care of the baby. One afternoon just as she was getting her son down for a nap, Gladys came down the hall looking worried.

"Syl, a Social Worker rapped on my door and wants to talk to you."

Last week, Vi warned Syl about this possibility. Her foreman Jake also shared a personal story: his sister's two-year-old girl was dragged from her mother's arms screaming and crying, never to return. After a terse conversation with the social worker, Syl left her baby in Gladys's care and rushed across the street to the True Love Café. Vi spotted Syl in the doorway.

"Grab the end booth hon, I'll be right down."

Vi quickly become a part of Syl's new makeshift family. Syl slid into the worn red leather booth. Comfortable, it was cracked with age and use. She watched Vi approach with two steaming cups of hot coffee.

"What's up, you're not looking too chipper."

Syl took a quick gulp of her coffee.

"Those bloody social workers found me. They showed up at Gladys' door."

Vi slid an ashtray towards Syl.

"Damn, I was hoping they'd leave you alone."

Vi stared out the window watching the snow accumulate on the pane.

"Do you have an extra smoke, mine are in the back?"

Syl tossed a rolled cigarette to Vi.

"Just when everything was going so well, I work my ass off to take care of my baby."

"What did you tell them?"

Vi reached over and lit Syl's smoke. The smell of sulphur rose between them, a comfort to Syl.

"Not much, somehow they knew I had a baby and wanted to know if I had a husband." Vi's eyes narrowed with anger.

"Women suffer the consequences, and to top it off men get the final say. It seems like we can't win."

For the first time Syl was concerned. She thought they'd go away and forget about her.

"No one's taking my baby, I'll go back up north and hide him if I have to."

Vi smiled at Syl's tenacious spirit.

"You still haven't told me, what did you tell them?"

"I lied. I said my husband was up north looking for a place for us."

Vi shook her head.

"Jesus Syl, now you've opened up a can of worms."

Syl bit her bottom lip.

"It's not like I had time to plan a speech, they caught me by surprise."

The bell door rang at the café. Vi jumped up to serve a regular, returning with two plates of food.

"Eat! Hank saw you come in and thought you were looking too skinny."

Syl picked at the fried potatoes, and greasy eggs. "I thought if I said, 'up north' they'd give up."

Vi chortled and took a gulp of her coffee.

"Don't kid yourself, those nosey bastards love to hunt down unwed mothers. The ones I've met are so bloody self-righteous and rigid." Syl pushed her plate away.

"Jake, my foreman, had a sister, who..."

Vi interrupted quickly.

"I told you that story. Tragic. She never recovered, and her little girl wasn't seen again." Syl shook her head.

"I can damn well tell you that's not happening to me. Jake asked me if there was anyone, I could fake it with in case something like this happened."

Vi was intrigued.

"Fake what, a marriage?"

Syl watched the snowflakes getting larger, leaving only a small opening in the window. Across the street, Gladys was caring for the infant she had obviously grown to love. He was oblivious to everything except comfort and warmth. Oblivious to the chain of events that would shape his life.

"It feels wrong. Hugh and I have plans."

Vi grabbed the ashtray and ground her cigarette against the glass.

"Yeah, well I can tell you, Jesus had plans too, and look what happened to him." "I just know I'll do anything to keep my baby. I'll write to Hugh and let him know. Do you really think they'll keep checking up on me?"

"Damn tooting they will."

Vi continued urging Syl to finish her food.

"Let's keep this simple, men are a dime a dozen, your kid won't cheat on you or wander off. He's going to be around the rest of your life. If you can find a decent guy willing to consider let's call it, a marriage of convenience..."

Syl surprised herself as she spoke.

"I'll talk to Jake. My choices are limited, I haven't told my parents, and I don't think I could just show up with a baby."

Vi and Syl walked arm in arm towards the door.

"Hang in there girl, sometimes life just boils down to a compromise."

Syl thought about her dilemma on her way to the docks. She remembered the tenuous time at the Salvation Army Home, how eager they'd been to take her into the fold. The knowledge that they took the girls' babies to put up for adoption, came as a cruel surprise.

People for the most part, minded their own business where Syl came from.

Jake spotted Syl as soon as she punched in for work. The small, striking brunette was hard to ignore. In spite of her good looks, Syl had proven to be hardier than many of the men who worked for him.

"Hey, what's up, you look like you're carrying a burden."

There was no usual smile or greeting from her today.

"Yeah, a big one."

She lowered herself onto to a stool and lit a cigarette.

"Are you and that soldier boy of yours having problems?"

Jake tried not to be too nosey. Syl blew a line out of the corner of her mouth.

"Yeah he's not here, and it doesn't seem to be happening any-time soon and we have a baby. It looks like I'll have to marry a stranger to keep him. That's a big burden."

"By God, have them damn welfare people found you and the kid again?"

Jake wrestled his cigarettes from his rolled-up shirt sleeve. Syl lit up her second one.

"That's about it. I'm scared shitless to leave him alone with Gladys."

"You'd need to find someone of good character who understands the situation. Let me think on this, Syl."

These were difficult times, especially for a woman. Hugh had a night of passion, Syl was left with a lifetime of consequences. Jake thought of her as the perfect sister: smart, beautiful and competent. Why were they bothering a woman like Syl? Why should she risk los-ing the child she worked hard and provided for, because she didn't have a marriage certificate? Jake promised to himself and silently to Syl, he would find a solution. The following week he stopped by her station with news.

"You free Friday after work, one of the fellas knows this guy who sounded interested." Syl felt momentary relief. It sounded simple. A piece of paper . . . but she knew men in a different way. What would he expect from her? After her shift Syl caught the trolley and went straight to her room. She lit up a smoke, leaning against the side of her only window. There was a loud ruckus outside.

"Give that back, you asshole, or I'll break it over your head."

Two drunks were fighting over a bottle of cheap booze in the alley.

"I'll give it to you alright, come closer and you'll get what you deserve."

Syl closed the thin white curtain and sat down on her bed. Syl promised Jake she'd meet him and the mystery man she could soon be calling her husband. Her letter to Hugh explaining the situation had been answered. Hugh said he understood and was waiting for the day they would be reunited. Syl had explained that this was a fake union, nothing but a marriage of convenience.

On Friday night Syl put on her best blouse. It was white with tiny flowers dotted across the bodice. She fluffed up her dark curls and used her red lipstick sparingly. She didn't want to appear too attractive. When she arrived at the small hall where the ship workers congregated after work Jake was waiting for her. He looked nervous. Syl noticed a young man sitting behind him. He sported a large head full of curly dark hair, and he didn't appear to be shy.

"Want to have a drink with your new husband?"

His smirk made Syl's stomach turn. Jake was visibly upset, avoiding Syl's glare. Syl gave John his first clue that she wouldn't be easy to tame.

"I don't drink and not bloody likely. You'd be a real compromise."

She began to walk away.

"Hey, you get to keep your kid."

John's smirk was gone. He had been discharged from the army, it was rumoured, because he had flat feet. His mother and father had all but given up on him. Later, after the hasty ceremony, John's mother would recount the story time and again. At the age of seven, how he ran and hid on the day of his first communion. That would be a sign of things to come. Syl was naive enough to think that John would honour their agreement to live together until Hugh returned. Within weeks, he insisted she meet his family. He shocked Syl by introducing the baby as his own. His family were welcoming. His father was rumoured to have sustained a head injury. This could have accounted for the difficult father he would become. John's youngest brother was at a private boys' school, and quick to comment on his brother.

"Did you know my pop calls my brother John, the black sheep?"

The words rolled easily off his younger brother's tongue as though they were often repeated.

In a short space of time, John's true colours emerged.

"Where'd you pick up that filthy smoking habit?"

Syl stood her ground in the beginning.

"With my brothers, behind the barn."

She could sense a simmering darkness in John. For a time, he worked hard to stay on his best behaviour, but not for long.

"Don't get lippy with me you no-good bitch, things are going to change around here." Syl went into her room and closed the door. It was no longer the safe and private space she had envisioned before the marriage. John had broken the lock the week before. The baby was crying, and Syl was frantically trying to soothe him.

"Can't you shut that bloody kid up?"

John's harsh voice penetrated the room. Syl didn't answer. John put all his weight against the door, knocking it open and destroying the barrier between them.

Syl jumped up, the baby in her arms.

"Get out, this is my room."

John narrowed his eyes at Syl, daring her to stand up for herself.

"Don't forget, you're under my roof, and you are my wife now."

How could she forget? He insisted she quit her job and see less of Vi and Gladys. Syl managed to send Hugh letters, taking them to the post office when John was at work. Gladys kept all of Hugh's when they arrived, and Syl read them there. While she still had hope he would return to her, if a letter was later than she expected, a feeling of doom enveloped her.

The inevitable happened. The war was coming to an end, and Syl discovered she was pregnant with John's child. She thought about leaving many times, but Social Services still had an eye on her, she suspected because of information from Effie at the Baywood. There was nowhere to go, and John's mother was welcoming to her and her young son. She had a suspicion his family sensed the tension between her and John. If they did, they kept it to themselves. Syl was gradually cut off from everything and everyone she'd known unless John approved.

Eventually, Hugh received word through the army circuit that Syl was expecting John's child.

Dear Hugh:

I can't wait until you are in my arms again. Our son looks just like his daddy. He even holds his head the way you do. His blonde curls and blue eyes are exactly like yours. I know there are rumours going around that I am expecting John's child. Don't believe any of them. John is a mean-spirited man. He's a bloody liar, and I can't wait to be away from him for good. My father has even offered to pay for a divorce. Remember that I love you. I am waiting for your return.

All my love, Syl and Sonny xox

My Darling Hugh: December 24, 1945.

Another Christmas Eve without you. Our son is strong and healthy. It's so cute when he puts his little hand on my face and tries to comfort me. I took an old parka apart and made him a winter coat. My former landlady, Gladys, sent him a wooden truck. Merry Christmas, and I hope next year the three of us can be together forever.

Your one true love, Syl xox

CHAPTER TWO

Syl's Return Home

Between trying to convince herself that she could tolerate John's violent outbursts, and periods where she could admit the truth, Syl decided to leave. Hugh's letters were coming to Gladys, and she would read them while John was at work. She mailed this last one to him, disclosing her plans. She didn't put her usual red kisses on the envelope not wanting the letter to attract attention.

My Darling Hugh: November 15, 1944.

I want you to know that I'm leaving on the train tomorrow with our baby. I am going to my folks up north, and you can write to me there. John's violence is getting worse. He is getting rough with the baby. John is a liar, and I can see now that he has no plans to let me go. As I have no money of my own since I stopped working, Gladys is giving me the train fare. There are rumours that the war is coming to an end soon. I hope that's true, so we can live as a family. Next time you hear from me, I will be safe, and far away from here.

All my love, Syl and baby.

The walk to the trolley would be a bit difficult. The baby wasn't walking yet. He was plump and healthy. Syl's small four-foot-nine-inch frame weighed about a hundred pounds. She dressed the baby in a light blue romper, yellow ducks strung across the bodice, slipped on her freshly ironed grey slacks and crisp white blouse, and pulled a red V neck over her dark hair. She packed a small suitcase for the two of them, knowing she'd need to replace things later. She grabbed the small green quilt Gladys made for the baby and pulled it around his chubby legs. With one last glance around the room, Syl walked out the door.

She boarded the trolley and sat at the back being cautious in case someone recognized her. That wasn't likely because she was rarely allowed to leave the apartment. John expected her to stay at home with the baby, her visits to Gladys and Vi severely limited.

"You've already done enough gallivanting, look at the mess you've made of your life so far."

Syl tried not to respond because she knew it would lead to a fight.

"Your job is to take care of me and the house. I expect the house to be spotless and a meal waiting for me when I walk through the door."

This was the price Syl paid for the roof over her head. He reminded her of it regularly.

"Let me help you with that baby," Syl was struggling with her suitcase.

An older woman on the trolley saw her struggling to pick the wriggling baby up. She quickly came to help. Syl made her way to the train station wicket. Although she knew that John was at work, and they'd be long gone before he returned home, the gnawing in her gut was still present. She sat on a wooden bench, waiting for the familiar rumble on the tracks. When the shrill whistle made the baby cry, she stuck a bottle in his trembling mouth, quieting him quickly. The kind stranger who'd helped her earlier boarded the train too. For the long train ride, they sat on seats facing one another. Soon the baby was lulled into a deep slumber, the familiarity of Gladys's quilt entwined in his little fingers.

Syl was thumbing through a McCall's magazine Gladys had given her for the trip. The kind stranger was alternately watching the city disappear, while glancing at Syl and the sleeping baby.

"I don't mean to pry, but are you going to meet your husband?"

Syl was taken aback for a minute but soon regained her composure.

"My husband, yes, yes, we are going to wait for my husband, up north."

"It sounds as though some of them will be returning home over the next few weeks."

The woman was shaking her head.

"My son, too, we are the lucky ones; at the very least, we are getting them back. Some not so lucky, or returning with such serious injuries, their lives will never be the same."

"Yes, my brothers too, I know that two will be returning soon, and still two at home," Syl replied.

"All we can do is pray," the kind stranger offered.

Syl nodded, although prayer was the furthest thing from her mind right now. The older woman clucked her tongue. She shook her head again at the realities that this war had visited on all of them.

"Well, that precious little fellow will soon have his daddy back, too, we can praise the Lord for that."

Syl didn't have the heart to tell her the truth, the baby and his father were about to meet for the first time. Her parents hadn't met him yet either. When Syl left they didn't know she was pregnant. There was no reason to alarm them while she was working. Now she wished she'd returned home when Social Services began to bother her.

She could have avoided this so-called marriage of convenience. Syl was independent. She had proven that she could take care of herself and her child. That was all that mattered.

Her family would see a different Syl now. She had settled down and the adversity had tempered her wild youthful exuberance. There was a new maturity to the young woman they'd last seen. Soon Syl and the kind stranger were both dozing, Syl sporadically conscious as mothers are, of the baby beside her, keeping one hand on his little leg.

When he awoke, she stood him on her knee and moved him closer to the window. Together they watched the telephone poles whizzing by. There was a rhythm to it, every clickity-clack of the train's wheels would equal five telephone poles left behind. It was a mirror image of Syl's descent into the city months before. Night was closing in on them, and soon she settled the baby back down on the seat. Softly and quietly, she rubbed his back and sang the song she'd sung to him every night since his birth.

'You are my sunshine, my only sunshine...'

Soon they were both sound asleep.

Syl woke up as the baby began to stir. She watched the sun rise over the distant hill, remembering the tranquillity here as a child. She was excited but also anxious about seeing her parents. Syl knew in her heart that they would be happy to meet their grandson. She would need to tell them that she wouldn't be returning to John. She'd written and explained the reason that she was marrying him. She did not include all the grim details. Nor did they know about her intention to reunite with her son's father when he returned from the war. As for the new life stirring in her belly, she was determined to keep it a secret until she could end it.

Familiar landmarks soon began to appear, the water tower looming over the trees at the base of the mountains.

That meant the station was only about forty minutes away. She began to gather the baby's things and the blue soft stuffed bunny that was a gift from Vi when he was born. She put a comb through her hair, said her goodbyes to her travelling companion and wished her well.

"I hope everything works out well for you and your son."

Syl folded the quilt and put it beside her. The kind stranger handed Syl the knitted sock that had fallen off the baby as he slept. Her stop was next, and they both waved, as her new friend stood outside on the platform. Syl took out her compact and applied some bright red lipstick. She checked herself in the mirror and snapped it closed. The baby had dribbled some milk on his chin; she wet her finger and wiped it clean. As the train began to slow down, there were alternate clangs and screeches. The steel on steel sparked its way to the station, grinding to a halt. Syl could see her two stay-at-home brothers were waiting anxiously by the station. They were parked on the side, waiting with a horse and plank wagon. It was a far cry from the noisy, modern city with its buses and trolleys and cars.

Her favourite brother Wallace reached her first. He embraced both Syl and the baby. Hoisting his new nephew on his shoulders, he was surprised at how small babies were.

"I'm going to be your favourite uncle."

He winked at his brother. The baby grabbed his uncles' hair and looked around at the new surroundings.

"Where's your luggage?"

Her brother Ray wasn't as friendly. He gave Syl a quick hug. There had always been a rivalry between them because Syl was as capable, more in some instances, as Ray working alongside their father.

"I only have the one suitcase."

She hoisted herself into the crude seat at the front of the wagon. The three of them managed to squeeze in, with Syl and the baby in the middle because there were no sides to protect them from falling off. The old horse plodded along the badly rutted makeshift roads, stopping every twenty feet or so to grab a fresh bunch of grass. Wallace had the reins, and every so often he would flap them in the air, click his tongue and say gently,

"Come on, old girl, move along."

Syl was enjoying the quiet, and taking in her childhood home: the mountains, the fields filled with yellow buttercups, and even the acrid smell of the sweaty horse as it moved them along. How foolish she'd been to give this all up. If she hadn't been so proud and stubborn she could have stayed, worked up the line, and one of her sisters would have helped with the baby. Wallace left her alone with her thoughts, but Ray wasn't as sensitive.

"So, how long you plan to stay?"

Syl readjusted the squirming baby on her knee. She took a deep breath before answering.

"I'm not going back."

Wallace just stared ahead. He was aware of the tension between his siblings.

"What the hell Syl, you're married, you can't just up and leave."

Syl knew that life was black and white to Ray. Wallace was different, she trusted him with her secrets. He had a sensitivity the other brother lacked.

"Well, I did, and it's no business of yours."

She knew there was no point trying to explain the situation to Ray. Her father would buffer her from his comments, once she had an opportunity to tell him the entire story.

The wagon pulled past Syl's old schoolhouse. Not much had changed. The grass was knee-high, but she knew the community would get together with their scythes and whack it down before school began in the fall. The paint was peeling on the wall of the outhouse where Syl had taken up smoking at the age of eleven.

The homestead was now visible, and the small figure in the distance was her father. He was eager to greet his daughter, the one who'd worked as well as her brothers on the farm. As they came closer, she watched him wipe his signature red handkerchief across his forehead. He met the wagon and took the baby from Syl as she jumped to the ground. His grandson took to his grandfather immediately, clutching him around the neck and inspecting the unfamiliar face. They would forge an unbreakable bond for the next few years.

"It's good to see you, Syl."

Her father patted her on the back.

"Yeah, and apparently she's not just visiting."

Ray was brooding and not thrilled that his younger sister, who had always shown him up, had returned home.

"Keep a lid on it, son."

On the walk up to the farmhouse, Syl recounted the past year to her father, how she was doing well until Social Services had threatened to take her baby, how she decided to enter the marriage of convenience, how she planned to reunite with Hugh when he returned from the war.

"Jeez, Syl, you can't be married to two men, what are you thinking?"

He shifted his new grandson to the other side and stared at the ground.

"John went back on his word and has been beating me. He's starting to rough up the baby, he doesn't like him."

"Well, I guess under those circumstances, you've done the right thing."

They'd stopped to catch their breath and her father sat down on a nearby stump, putting the baby on the ground. The child had never been on the ground before and was examining the grass, pulling bits out and trying to eat them.

"What are you going to do about this marriage, Syl?"

Syl lit a cigarette, staring off towards the familiar mountains. Her father, William, watched his young grandson crawl on the field. Eagles were flying overhead, searching for prey.

"Why would a grown man hit a woman, or a baby?"

The child's blond curls fell over his forehead as he alternately picked at the flowers, glancing up at the noisy birds in the open sky.

"He's not a man, daddy. John forgets why we are together. He treats me like he owns me." Syl smoked as though her life depended on it. They were both silent for a few minutes while they concentrated on the child. His grandfather marvelled at the child's glee with new discoveries. He was a welcome diversion from the realities of the mess Syl had created.

Her father looked puzzled.

"Why didn't you just come home?"

And then another question:

"If Hugh knew you were expecting his child, why didn't he marry you before he left?"

Syl was silent, but she wasn't sure about that either.

"What about this John's family, I thought they were decent, educated people?"

"He doesn't show the bad side to them, but they do refer to him as the black sheep of the family."

"You said they were good Catholics, but I suppose religion doesn't make everyone honourable." He continued as though in this peaceful place with the clear blue spacious skies, a solution they hadn't thought of could fall from the heavens. Syl's father spotted her brothers walking across the field after putting the horses away.

"Ray was already giving me attitude on the ride over. I don't need any shit from him right now."

Her father nodded towards the child.

"Watch your mouth, Syl," and after another long pause, "What about the child's father?" Syl took a deep breath.

"He's meeting me at the station on Wednesday, he's not discharged yet from the army, but they're letting him come home on leave. I didn't want to say too much in front of Ray."

"Pay no mind to Ray, I've picked him up a few times when he's fallen in the mire, not that I can complain, I can't run this place by myself."

Her brothers arrived back from putting the horses away. They both watched the baby playing on the grass. Her father turned to Syl once he saw the boys were engaged with their nephew.

"I hate to tell you this, but there is more bad news."

Syl had never seen her father's eyes well up.

"What's wrong, is it one of the girls?"

Syl had been close to her two younger sisters and was anxious to see them again.

"Not the girls, your mother, they're talking about sending her to the institution on the coast."

"The institution! Why would they send her there?"

Syl was shocked at the news. Her mother had always appeared to be so strong, and she never imagined that anything could happen to her. She was supposed to grow old with her father, she had weathered so many events in her life.

"Well, they say she needs to be somewhere like that, near the end."

Syl grabbed her father's hand.

"Jesus, Daddy, she's not dying, is she?"

Syl couldn't imagine life without her mother somewhere. Her father removed his box of chewing tobacco, took a pinch and stuck it behind his bottom lip. He was quiet as was his habit, and when he spoke, Syl's world fell apart.

"They say there's a snowball's chance in hell, she'll live for another year."

Syl pulled the velvety buttercup apart, the yellow staining her fingers.

"You said she had headaches."

"Turned out to be a brain tumour, nothing they can do, nothing we can do but wait, we're going to lose her, Syl."

"Does she know how bad it is?"

Syl had almost lost her ability to breathe.

"She knows, but you know your mother, she takes care of everyone else first. The girls are young, they just know she is sick."

Her father leaned over and took a buttercup from his grandson's mouth.

"Let's go up to the house and see your mother, she's been waiting for you."

Syl was shocked at her mother's appearance. She looked to be half the weight she was when Syl had last seen her. Syl hugged her carefully and held onto her much longer than usual. Her mother too, took to her new grandchild, and offered him a biscuit. Soon the girls arrived home and the house buzzed with chatter. Syl's father drew her aside later in the evening when all had quieted down, and the baby was fast asleep.

"I'll take the train into town tomorrow and find a lawyer. I will see if there is anything we can do about this mess. I'm not sure that it's a good idea for Hugh to be showing up here right now."

"John's not the husband I wanted. I have no feelings for him other than dread."

Wednesday arrived and Syl waited alone at the station. She'd set her hair the night before in bobby pins and it was a halo of thick dark curls. The train pulled slowly into the station. Hugh's anxious face was pressed against the window. His big grin told Syl that there was nothing to worry about. He jumped off quickly and grabbed his girl up in his arms.

"I can't believe I'm here."

They hugged as though it would last forever.

"You are, and in about twenty minutes you're going to meet our baby. He has your blond curls and blue eyes. He looks even more adorable than he does in his pictures."

Together they walked slowly across the field. The Selkirk Mountains sloped in the distance and the dense forest lay at their feet. Syl remembered the nights they'd spent lying as lovers in this field for lack of privacy anywhere else. Today she had rejected her brother's offers to bring the wagon, not wanting to share these first precious moments with anyone but Hugh.

Back at her parents' log house, her sisters were preparing the baby to meet his father for the first time. They wet his blond curls and dressed him in his mother's favourite romper. He was like a dress-up doll to the two girls.

The walk gave Hugh and Syl the first chance to talk in person in a long time. They talked about Syl's choice to enter the marriage she didn't want in order to keep their son.

"Now he has taken over everything in my life. I can't see my friends and am accountable to him for everything."

Hugh was quiet for a few moments and then he had to raise the forbidden subject he'd hinted at in a recent letter.

"I heard through others overseas, who know him, that you are pregnant with his child."

Syl could see how complicated this had become and the lie came easily from her.

"Well, he's a goddamn liar, I was beat up when I tried to stand up for myself." Hugh let the subject drop. He was just happy to be back in his own country and soon to be discharged from the army. Syl was relieved, confident that she could deal quietly with the awkward organism growing inside her. They walked arm in arm, talking about the war, the devastation and the boys who weren't returning home. Syl recounted her experience as a welder and riveter on the warships in Vancouver, stories she'd told him in her letters.

"The war wasn't easy for any of us."

As they neared the house Syl could see that the girls had the baby on the front porch. He was a small replica of his father, and there was no doubt they were father and son. Hugh was straining his neck to get a better look and then broke into a run. His experience with babies and small children was limited, and the suddenness of his approach made the baby cry.

"Shhh... that's your daddy."

Syl was determined that they would bond and that her fantasy of the perfect family she wanted would soon come true. Eventually, the baby crawled over to his daddy, and they began what would be a short-term relationship as father and son, their future mired in lies and complications that even Syl's determination couldn't overcome.

Syl's family pulled out all the stops for Hugh's visit. They were happy to see him, but the complication of Syl's marriage hung like a dark storm, brewing amidst the clear blue skies. Her father tried to be comforting.

"I can see how happy he makes you, and every child should grow up with his real daddy.

I'll do my best to help sort this out, Syl."

Syl and her father were close. Syl was like a little Annie Oakley, could handle a rifle, shoot bears, and tromped in the outdoors with her father as a child.

At the same time, her brothers learned to cook. It was a well-adjusted family, better than most. Syl's parents were well regarded in the small community, always ready to lend a helping hand.

The reality of time passing was weighing heavily on Syl. She took picture after picture of the child with his daddy.

"Go stand over there now, lean him up by your leg."

Her father took photographs of the three of them, the perfect family that really wasn't, and would never be. Syl wanted the happiness of that reunion to be captured for all time. The morning for Hugh to return to the barracks arrived, and once again, Syl refused the offer of the wagon. She knew that the walk home would be long and lonely, but she needed time alone to take care of the trepidation she knew she'd be feeling.

The train was waiting at the station when they arrived. Two young lovers had brought a child into the world and dreamed of becoming a family. Their youth, both in their early twenties, gave them the freedom to let thoughts go, to not examine the ugly reality that had been created. In a sense they were still living in the moment, the same moment that had created their child. The need to close their eyes to consequences was apparent, even during this reunion. By the intervention of fate and circumstance, they would never meet again.

"All aboard."

The conductor was giving his final shout. He was accustomed to these small-town stops, where lovers and husbands were either arriving or leaving, reluctant to say that last goodbye. Syl ran alongside the train, while Hugh's face was pressed once more against the window. A memory of arriving and leaving, forever to be etched in Syl's memory. The train lurched and the wheels sparked, the whistle announcing its final farewell. Syl fell back, breathless and began the long walk home.

Her father had caught her alone earlier with some news.

"There was a telegram from John this morning, he's coming here to take you back." There would be no more promises of heroic legal interventions from her father after that telegram arrived. Her father's mind was on the impending demise of his wife.

Syl stopped near her old schoolhouse and sat on a weathered bench. She had memories of sitting here as a child, trading homemade bread with raisins for plain bread with her friend. At this moment she wished that childhood has lasted longer, and she hadn't been in such a hurry to become an adult. She thought back to all the times she and her friends tried to peer far into an unknown future. They discussed the lives they envisioned, the wonderful husbands they would marry, and the beautiful children they would have. They were all grown-up words for a world they couldn't wait to taste. Syl, in particular, pushed for adulthood.

Her good looks and tomboy charm made her popular. She was feisty as a girl and independent. Her inability to make good decisions as a young adult would rule the rest of her life. Too late, she realized that her parents had been right.

"Slow down, Syl, and enjoy your childhood."

Sitting on the bench, Syl had flashbacks to the days of summer as a child. She would meet her friends here, there would be much laughing and bravado as they smoked their homemade cigarettes. Neither of her parents smoked, and they were horrified when they found out. Syl pulled her pack of cigarettes out and lit one. She revelled in the semi-silence of this desolate wilderness she'd grown up in. There was always a rustle in the bushes, rabbits, foxes and deer. The bears were usually deeper in the bush and were more than likely to be hunted rather than predatory.

Syl walked towards the house. She still hadn't had time to digest the fact that her mother was dying. One year, she was going to miss out on her grandchild, and he would never remember her. The implications of those losses fell heavily on Syl. Her sisters were still in school. What would they do without their mother? She put those sad thoughts aside, just as she had put aside the complicated life she had created, dreaming instead about the fanciful but impossible future she wanted with Hugh. The birds began to squawk and fly erratically, and Syl could see that a storm was coming. She moved quickly and made it to the front porch just as the lightning cracked across the summer sky. She now regretted she'd told John anything about her life and her family. He constantly brought up the fact that the child wasn't his.

"You're nothing but a slut."

He knew he wasn't her first choice or her choice at all, and he never let her forget it. She'd never been around men who treated women the way he did. Where she came from, girls and boys were treated as equals. Her parents had instilled that in them from an early age. Her parents had always been a team, raising their children, preparing food and meat for winter, managing their simple day-to-day lives.

Syl's father had laid his own mother to rest in the crude local cemetery just two years before. His young son, Lawrence, Syl's brother, who had drowned in the Fraser River at the age of nine, was buried beside her. Now the thought of his beloved wife lying in the cold ground beside them, was unbearable. He hoped the doctors were wrong, and a miracle would come to pass when she went to the institution where patients with brain tumours were sent to live out their lives. It was four days of travel on the train. He couldn't imagine his young daughters so far away from their mother and them growing up without her.

John had sent the telegram while Hugh was visiting. Syl's father made up excuses as to why he should wait a day or two. But John was stubborn and said he would arrive on the train that morning.

"She's my wife, and I have a right to come and take her back."

When Syl arrived back at the house her sisters were laughing and playing with their young nephew. She watched as they took turns, hiding behind an easy chair, and then popping out. He would break into gales of laughter and roll on the floor. He'd finally begun to stand on his own, and his chubby legs would buckle as he laughed and reached out for them. Syl had never seen her son so relaxed and happy. The tension of living with John never left them. When he was away at work, there was the knowledge that he would return.

John arrived with none of the fanfare of Hugh's visit a week earlier. John was a simmering person, his outbursts were sudden and violent, with no warning. In the moments between, he was a silent man. Silent and forbidding, unpredictable, a menacing presence that Syl would live with for a great part of her life, and that would be inflicted on her children yet to be born.

Syl going to work at the shipyards as a riveter.

Longworth, BC train station

Hugh and Syl in Longworth, BC

Syl with Mother.

CHAPTER THREE

My Home by The Fraser

My mother's constant humming was a source of comfort to me. She would hum quietly to herself or sing an odd line or a few words from a song.

On a hill far away stood... then she would hum. I knew it was The Old Rugged Cross, because sometimes she alternated, humming the beginning, then singing the ending. Sometimes it was, My Home by The Fraser. They were both sad, mournful songs that must have made her think about death, loss, and her past and future.

My Home by the Fraser arrived the same year that I did, 1946. A year later it outsold Bing Crosby's White Christmas. It was a song about a river, the longest in Canada, a river from my childhood memories, and for two uncles, a river of death.

I was three years old and had survived my mother's attempts to get rid of me. I pushed my way into a family deep in conflict, the first child of a union made in hell. John moved north, our log house was beside the raging Fraser River, surrounded by the Selkirk Mountains. The story of my birth was repeated many times over the years, always ending with the astonishment of all witnesses.

"You were so small, we had to warm you on the oven door, we weren't sure if you would survive the night."

My mother's secret was intact to all but a few.

My aunt, who was seventeen when I was born, told me I slept in her doll cradle. I remember my mother warning my brother, who was two years older, to hold my hand and watch out for the grizzly bears. I have photograph of me standing in a field, the snow a contrast to my red coat with matching leggings and hat, trimmed in white rabbit fur. Only five and three, we would walk along the fence line to visit our grandfather. I remember him carving me my first doll out of wood. Our grandmother died of her brain tumour, far out on the West Coast, when I was a baby. I never knew her. Our grandfather left us when I was three. My brother was so distraught, my mother said, he tried to jump into the grave with him. He would be the only father figure he would know.

Shortly after that, we moved to Vancouver. My mother was expecting my sister and wanted to have her in a hospital. We moved into a new post-war house that no one had ever lived in, with money from our grandfather's estate. My father planted the lawn we weren't allowed to walk on, and the flowers we couldn't pick, and a different way of living began. We no longer had to fear the Grizzly bears, now only our father.

Soon after we moved in, I heard the words I'd remember that would stay with me for years to come, only coming into focus many years later.

"I'm going to tell her what you did."

Those words would haunt me for four decades. My parents were arguing and as usual I was hovering at a safe distance. The words came from my father. I don't remember if my mother replied. I just knew that those words had something to do with me. I was sure that my life was predictably uncertain, contingent. I must always stay away from my father because I never knew what would make him angry. Throughout the years, my mother would tell me over and over.

"When you were a baby standing in your crib, you would shake when you heard his voice."

My sister's birth ushered in a new set of dynamics. My oldest brother was my mother's love child, clearly her favourite. I came next, the glue that held this ill-fated marriage together.

Another brother was born between me and my sister. By this time, I was self-sufficient and had no expectations from anyone. I asked my mother a lot of questions for a four-year-old.

"Why can't we move away from him?"

"We have nowhere to go."

She was alone in the world, with only her children to make her happy, when she had time to notice them. Her love showed when she knit us sweaters, mittens, and made us winter coats. Her needs were simple. Her parents were deceased and her siblings had lives of their own. One day she found me sobbing and wanted to know what I was going on about.

"I'm sad that your parents are dead."

I was already thinking about loss. My mother wanted no part of my sadness.

"Don't be ridiculous."

Then she looked at me and said the second thing I could never forget.

"I wonder if you're the way you are because…"

The rest of her sentence hung in the air. From that day forward I had a sense that she thought there was something wrong with me. I felt certain she was right, I didn't fit in.

I knew my mother had good memories of her own childhood. She always spoke lovingly of her parents. She'd set trap lines with her father, and he taught her to hunt and fish. Horses were the only daily mode of transport in their isolated community, so everyone knew how to ride.

It was a place she remembered fondly, and a family that protected and confirmed who you were. By contrast, I learned to hum early and understood why my mother might have done so. I hummed at night, my head under the covers to shut out the angry voices that had become the soundtrack of my life. With every passing year I became increasingly aware of who I wasn't. I knew that I lived in fear and wasn't safe.

My one saving grace was that my mother was a voracious reader. Before I started school, children's magazines would arrive in the mail. The first ones were Humpty Dumpty, then Jack and Jill. I devoured them. My mother showed me how to sound out letters and I learned to read very quickly. The short poems and stories helped me survive. Once I discovered the world of words, I didn't feel so isolated.

My first attempts at writing began when I was seven. I wrote letters to my mother. I wrote all the things I couldn't say to her face. I wrote about my feelings, trying to reach that part of her that was shut off. I was too young to know her story or the reasons she was always so sad. I knew my letters touched her, because I would watch her reaction after she'd read a letter. Often there would be tears in her eyes.

After the children's magazines, a series of children's classics began to arrive. Heidi, A Child's Christmas in Wales, and many others. They were bound in a deep rich burgundy leather. My love of books and reading began early. Not long after I began school, the teacher asked my mother to come and see her.

"Your daughter reads everything in sight."

My mother didn't understand what the fuss was about. She was concerned I was in trouble when she was asked to see the teacher, but that would come soon enough. "I taught her to read, she always has her face in a book."

Mrs. Kergan asked my mother's permission to allow me to help teach the slow readers. Before long, my small group of three, The Bears, sat in a semicircle in front of me. I was six years old.

By the time I was nine I'd become a source of entertainment for my class, and I was every teacher's worst nightmare. School had already become boring for me. I couldn't concentrate on much except thinking, at the end of the day I would have to go back home.

Syl with Sonny

Syl's twin brother Ernest and Megan

Sonny and Megan in the fields in Longworth BC.

Sonny and Megan as baby

Megan and sibling in Longworth BC

Syl and John with Megan

The Body Remembers

The body remembers the nights

the shutters banged.

Harsh winter wind insufficient to

disguise words flying like bullets.

The green of my room and Hans Brinker,

Tucked safely away, my only comfort.

A family in the midst of war,

children taken hostage lying

under cover waiting for the still.

Leaving me a discarded shell

stranded on a barren landscape,

Unlike those children

Smiling in my picture books.

CHAPTER FOUR

The Crazy Bastard

I was seven the year President Eisenhower boldly informed the Chinese that he wouldn't think twice about using weapons to end a conflict. Conflict wasn't new to me, and my parents could have given the Chinese a run for their money. I'd learned how to hold my breath waiting for the next explosion. My mother had it all figured out and did her best to control his violent outbursts. Our lives appeared normal until he arrived home. Dinner would be waiting, because he demanded it the minute he walked through the door. As the time of his arrival drew nearer, the tension in the house was palpable. There was a checklist to ensure that everything went smoothly.

"Make sure his paper is folded and on his end table, my mother would remind me."

I waited every day for the Vancouver Sun to arrive, and would read the stories voraciously, then put the paper back together without folding or creasing any of the pages. When his car pulled into the driveway, we would all scramble out of sight until we were called to the table for dinner. Our house was new, in a pleasant suburb. Our front yard was our father's pride and joy. It sprouted new grass and freshly planted flowers. The lawn was off limits to us. It only appeared in family photographs when aunts, uncles and cousins came to visit. We would line up for the camera and smile, as though standing on our father's lawn was the most normal thing in the world, his words ringing in our ears.

"I told you to stay to hell off that grass."

He was a tyrannical control freak. The house was his, the grass was his, and by the grace of God, he'd put a roof over our heads. He made it clear that it was by his permission that we were allowed to sit at the table and eat the food he worked to supply. Dinner was always in silence, no conversation.

"If I want to hear you speak, I'll let you know."

Agility was necessary to keep out of his way and my mother was always trying to run interference.

"Leave those kids alone or I'll tell your mother."

My mother knew the power of my grandmother, Elizabeth's presence. She was a diminutive, outspoken Irish woman, staunchly Catholic, and not to be underestimated. Born in Ireland, she grew up in England, and she had served her country during the First World War. She was awarded two medals for her service.

My mother held her tongue as much as she could, and on the occasions that she couldn't, there were consequences. He had a ritual, and we all knew the drill. Line his shoes up where he kicked them off at the door, eat dinner in silence, and make his tea. He would move from the table to his chair in the living room, his newspaper waiting, as far as he knew untouched.

Nothing was ever good enough.

"How long does it take to make a cup of tea?"

My mother would pour the milk and add two teaspoons of sugar into his cup. We were too young to be of much help and our presence annoyed him, so my mother would work from sunrise to sunset. Occasionally I would chance getting up very early. My mother would be sitting at the kitchen table rolling cigarettes from her can of Vogue tobacco. I'd stand and watch her, feeling her despair. As she blew the smoke into blue rings, she would stare blankly out the window, watching the sun rise. I would creep quietly back to my room, carrying the sadness of her lifelong burdens. Those were the only times I ever saw her sitting. She never sat at the table to eat with us, and I never saw her in bed. While we ate our breakfast, she leaned by the kitchen counter and picked at her food. After she got the crazy bastard, as she referred to him, out the door, there were kids to get off to school, and more work to be done.

The year I turned seven, pleated skirts were in vogue. My favourite was the one with all the colours of the rainbow, a sign of things to come. Row upon row of micro-pleats; when I twirled, my underpants would show, but I didn't care. That was the year my grandmother took me to mass at her Catholic church, and to see the ballet, The Red Shoes. I loved the pageantry of the church, Jesus hanging from a cross while Mary, his mother wept. I pretended I knew when to kneel and pray. My mother had a different view.

"They're just a bunch of bloody hypocrites, you know they think we're going to hell, and that we are all heathens."

No matter, it was one place I could feel at peace.

That was the year I made a memory with my mother, just the two of us. She had little time for luxury and didn't drive, so everything was ordered from the Sears & Roebuck's or Eaton's catalogues. When those volumes arrived, I would study them for hours, circling the things I hoped to have. Sensible and long-lasting shoes were what I usually got, but I longed for a pair of red leather Mary Jane's. Somehow, she knew how important they were to me, and one day, with no prior discussion, we caught the bus to Copps' shoe store on Columbia Street in New Westminster, just the two of us. That night I slept with my new red shoes, one tucked on either side of my face so I could smell the leather. I wore them until I had to put cardboard in the bottom.

That summer Queen Elizabeth was crowned in England, and my mother lost a chunk of her beautiful black hair, and two teeth. The night had started out as normal as any in our home, but my mother sensed friction as soon as he entered the house.

"Don't you think you could have dinner on the table when I walk through the door?" My mother could tell he was itching for an argument. She remained silent and was scurrying about, mashing the potatoes and grabbing a baby who was about to fall out of his highchair. She had a cigarette on her bottom lip taking an occasional drag when she could.

"When are you going to quit that filthy habit?"

This was the year the experts reported that cigarette smoking was directly related to cancer. My mother was resigned.

"Everyone has to die of something."

That night it could have been her. After a tense dinner, the tea ritual was repeated. A kettle fully boiled, the taste test, to make sure it was exactly hot enough, exactly sweet enough. My mother was trying to remove the mashed potatoes from the baby's hair and asked my brother to take the tea to the living room. My father had inherited his British father's rigidity, not his Irish mother's pleasant disposition. He would only drink his tea from a thin china cup and saucer. My brother walked slowly, balancing the hot cup of tea, the rattle of the cup the only noise in the silence.

"Get a move on, it'll be cold before you get here."

His words jolted my brother, and he attempted to move faster. As he was about to set the cup and saucer on the end table beside the newspaper, all hell broke loose. The cup tipped; the tea spilled all over the headlines.

'Polio Vaccine Trials to Begin.'

The cup crashed to the floor and shattered, and my brother began to shake.

"What in the hell did you do that for?"

Just as my brother was ducking to avoid a harsh blow, my mother stepped between them.

"For Christ's sake, leave him alone, he's just a kid."

She bent over and began to pick up the pieces and shooed us out of the way.

"Go to your rooms before you get glass in your feet."

I sensed danger and hovered in the hallway, watching and listening. She was trying to appease the crazy bastard.

"I'll get this cleaned up and make you another cup of tea." He wasn't in a mood to be appeased.

"What about my paper, how am I supposed to read it now?"

My mother was now crouched on all fours, the pink and green flowers of the Royal Albert scattered across the floor. It happened quickly, but the scene remained frozen in my mind for decades. With horror, I watched him grab my mother by the hair, and drag her screaming across the floor.

"Let me go, you crazy bastard, you're hurting me."

That just added fuel to the inferno.

"Crazy eh, crazy, I'll show you crazy."

With that, he picked up her small four-foot-nine body, smashing her head into the living room wall. The impact left a hole in the drywall. She repaired it herself the next day. That was the moment I realised I could never love my father. I lost hope that I would ever be able to find, or feel, normal.

The following month, the coronation of Queen Elizabeth was a big deal. We were given coins in class to commemorate the event. Our school was staging a May Day celebration and I was one of the girls chosen to take part as a flower girl. I was assigned a pale green, flocked nylon dress with puffed sleeves, and a wreath of green flowers for my hair. I had a childlike feeling my luck was about to change. What ruined it was the fact that my father had to escort me. I waved cautiously to my family as we drove off in the grey Plymouth. After the ceremony the flower girls danced around the Maypole, and the music began to start the evening. The flower girls were supposed to enter the dance floor with their fathers for the first dance. I flatly refused. My father was someone I feared, and the thought of pretending he was the kind of father I could dance with was too much for me. We drove home in silence, because with him silence was my habit.

A few weeks later, he made me pay for his humiliation that night. Summer was on the way, and the days were getting longer. We lived on a street where children could play with no concern for their safety. We could roller-skate, play tag and walk with bare feet on hot pavement. We were usually sent to bed directly after dinner, depending on my father's mood. We would lie in bed listening to the neighbourhood children laughing and playing while the sun went down. My younger sister and I slept in a double bed, and we would never risk anything above a whisper, but sometimes even that was too much for him. On this particular night he burst through the door with no warning, belt in hand.

"Didn't I tell you that I didn't want to hear from you?"

The belt rose over his head, buckle side down. He lashed as hard as he could, until my legs were cut and bleeding, and I was begging him to stop. My mother was standing in the doorway yelling at him.

"Leave the little one alone."

She was referring to my sister, who was lucky enough to be beside the wall.

When he finished the lashing, I was left in bed, the wounds stinging and bleeding, my face buried deep in my pillow so I could cry silently. By morning the cuts were beginning to fester, and there was no mention of the beating. I knew enough to keep my pain to myself.

It's curious that I gave no thought at the time to my mother's attempt to protect my sister, but not me. I was already resilient and had no expectations of protection from anyone. At seven, my inner and outer armour left me feeling empty inside. I promised myself that I would trust no one. Every year I coveted the metal dollhouse advertised in my brother's Archie comics. I wanted to create my life within those tin walls.

There is a strength within children that can move them forward. Their reality is the normal they know. Sometimes it can take years for the scars that have been hidden inside to surface. My life with the crazy bastard was just a small part of who I would become.

Megan with Grandfather (William)
and Uncle Peter

Megan in Longworth at age 3

Megan's 2nd birthday in Longworth with
Siblings and from left back row Aunt Helen,
Syl, and Aunt Alberteen.

John and Megan with 2
siblings

Megan age 2 in Longworth BC

*Megan with Birthday
Cake - age 4*

I Never See You Whole

You are

A small white harp,

A burial plot.

You are

A Mound,

fresh black dirt.

I never see you whole.

Your small glasses,

brittle with age

strong round frames

and one broken arm.

I never see you whole.

You, a small white harp

and I,

once a child,

who lost you in memory.

CHAPTER FIVE

Surviving Childhood

When we first moved into our Vancouver house, it stood in the middle of a mound of dirt in the front, and a large pile of builders' debris in the back. The wood pile was off limits, but what an alluring mountain of rubble it was for curious three and four-year-olds.

"Stay away from that woodpile, there are nails in there, and God knows what else." When my mother was busy punching the bread dough or putting the clothes through the wringer washer, we would explore. My early memories of my mother's appearance didn't match the photographs of an attractive young woman dressed up. She looked regal with her with her dark hair swept up on top of her head. The mother I knew wore jeans and a plaid shirt. There was always a shirt pocket to hold her cigarettes and lighter or matches; she rolled her own. The first house is where I watched my father rip out her hair and knock out her teeth before he slammed her head into the wall. It was where I saw Tinker-bell fly around the Disney castle, on our first black-and-white television. It was the house where the visiting nurse put a 'Quarantine' sign on our front door because we all had the measles. It was the house where I began grade one. I ran like hell past St. Helen's churchyard and cemetery every morning. It was the house where I wore my Dale Evans outfit on Halloween and saved all the candies wrapped in orange and black paper for my mother.

"MMM…those are my favourite."

She would chew on them like a child, her false teeth clicking up and down. On occasion she'd have to remove them to dislodge a wad of sticky Halloween candy. This was where I began Daily Vacation Bible School, and wondered where God was when I needed help. This street was the one where my younger siblings followed behind me to Sunday school to the echo of my mother's warning:

"Don't let the little ones too close to those ditches, the last thing I need is one of you drowning. Somewhere in that pavement are my crude carved initials. I can remember those lazy summer days before the sun was ready to fall behind the houses, the light shifting between the trees, and the smell of hot pavement, melted enough at the edges so I could stick my toes in. This was where I made my first friend, Judy Larson. She lived in a house across the street, the only house with a flat roof. Judy and I played with our dolls on her long driveway and when we could get away with it, watched the caps from our Dale Evans cap guns explode under rocks. Her mom was a nurse, so anytime I had a scrape she'd hoist me onto her kitchen counter.

"Let's look at that nasty cut."

While the thought of a bear didn't faze me, I wasn't brave when it came to cuts. I'd squeeze my eyes closed.

"Tell me when it's over."

Parry's grocery store was on the corner. We could get a double-decker ice-cream cone for five cents or one returned milk bottle. This is the first house I lived in where I realised at any moment my father could take me away from everything I loved, my first real friend.

"Your dad wants to buy a bigger house when school's out."

My best friend Judy was my first thought.

"How far are we going?"

My mother lit a cigarette and it hung on her bottom lip while she took the clothes off the line.

"Be damned if I know, he said he's going to look on the weekend."

My eight year old brain was trying to process losing the most important person in the world to me, at that time.

"Will I still be able to play with Judy?"

Judy and her family were my respite from my real life.

"There's no point in asking me questions I don't have the answers for."

My mom tossed the clothes pegs into a canvas bag and draped a bundle of diapers over my arm.

"Quit talking and carry these into the house."

I would be leaving behind the school where I impressed the teacher in Grade One with my reading skills, and where I got the strap, because for one entire week I was too terrified to speak to my father and ask for thirty-five cents. My mom was in the hospital having a baby, almost an annual event by now. I'd been warned by my teacher repeatedly, and humiliated in front of my class:

"You need to bring in thirty-five cents by Friday for your Think and Do workbook, or you are getting the strap, this is your last chance."

I was eight years old and what did I know about chances? Friday morning was my last chance day. I finally worked up enough nerve to speak to my father. I wondered if I should start with it being my last chance, or the money. It wasn't the money it was his need to control. Finally, I just spit it out.

"I need to take thirty-five cents to school or I'm going to get the strap."

I was staring at the Shell gas station calendar on the wall trying to avoid looking at him. The blonde woman sitting on the convertible in the picture looked right at me. I saw the large red circle around Monday. That meant my mom wouldn't be home in time to help me.

"What in the hell do you think we are, millionaires?"

I walked away and went to school. I knew I'd have to face my teacher in front of my class. Sure enough, right after roll call the teacher called me up.

"Well miss, I sure hope you remembered to ask for your Think and Do Money."

I looked her square in the eye.

"What in the hell do you think we are, millionaires?"

My classmates' eyes were wide as the strap was laid across my small hand, and I didn't even flinch. I was becoming immune to pain along with my feelings.

It didn't take long for me to lose interest in school. My grade four teacher disliked me, and I knew it. She kept getting my name mixed up with another girl in the class. That was proof of my insignificance. I was bored, and because school was the only place I was able to have any freedom, I could be like a hungry wolf with a rabbit. One day the class had painstakingly cut out fruit, using coloured construction paper. The matching paper bowl required a small slit to insert the fruit. I jumped onto the top of my desk when the teacher left the room and held a fruit auction. I'd turned into the class clown. The stakes were low for me at school. At home I couldn't speak out; at school I could swear like a sailor, and act like a jackass.

I was homely. My hair was straight, and my bangs were jagged up to my forehead. Before my mother cut my bangs they were hanging over my eyes. My two front teeth protruded, and I rarely smiled. School held one humiliation after another, all reminding me that I wasn't worthy.

One day my mom's oldest sister, my Aunt Thelma, was visiting and I risked asking her:

"Do you think I'm pretty?"

"No, you're not at all what I would call pretty, but you're not bad-looking either."

Most of my school memories after grade one were unpleasant. The walk to and from school, up until grade three, was terrifying. School was about a mile from our house, and every day I cringed knowing I had to walk by St. Helen's Cemetery. The old church was on the corner just before the curve. From there I walked down a steep hill to General Montgomery Elementary. Beginning in grade one, my father told me that I needed to run fast past the graveyard, or ghosts would come out and chase me. I would search the spaces between the rows of large white crosses and headstones in fear of spotting one. For years after, I had a recurring nightmare that I was trying to crawl from one side of that road to the other, always waking up just before a disaster. While the shutters banged in the wind against my bedroom window, I hummed, my head under the pillow. The loud angry voices of my parents would be muffled, replaced by the shutters and the howl of the wind. For some reason, at night alone in my room, the wind frightened me. Tucked beside me would be a book. 'Hans Brinker, or the Silver Skates,' or, 'Five Little Peppers and How They Grew.' I read that last story over and over, about a family whose father had died. The story gave me hope that everyone could have a happy ending. The single mother was left with five children, and they lived in their little brown house filled with love and laughter. At night the children would be lovingly tucked into bed by their mother. In spite of her circumstances, she laughed and danced with her children. One father gone, it was what I wished for.

We left our first house across from Judy's and moved to a new one. It was close to my school and my three cousins lived not far from me. Teresa, Monica, and Stewart, were my Aunt Mary's children from my father's side of the family, the only cousins close to our ages who lived nearby. We found an abandoned car behind the field at their house and spent hours traveling to far-off places. We called it the Deutenburger and took turns pretending to drive. We made up stories about where we were going and the places we would visit. We lived near the Vancouver Golf Club, and another fun pastime was looking for wayward golf balls on the side of the street. My aunt Mary was very kind to us, and I could see that she felt conflicted about her brother and how harsh he was with his children. But my aunt, like everyone in those days, turned a blind eye.

That year, my school thought it would be a great idea to hold a contest aimed at group humiliation. All the grade five girls were going to parade in front of the school in their finest dresses. The girl voted the prettiest would be the winner. Stephanie was our teacher's pet. Her long perfect ringlets bounced every time she sashayed down the hall. Her father dropped her off at school every morning in his shiny Black Mercury. He would jump out, open her door like she was some kind of princess. After he leaned down and kissed the top of her perfect hair, the black fins of the car would disappear. No one liked her except the teacher. Stephanie's clothes also set her apart. The majority of us wore sensible clothes to school: pleated wool skirts, jumpers with crisp white blouses, and shoes that would take us through a season. But every day was special for Stephanie. Her shoes were black patent sling-backs with shiny black bows on top. Her hair ribbons always matched her dress.

Somewhere in my subconscious, I had a fantasy that I could win the beauty contest. Maybe if I wore a beautiful dress, my limp hair and protruding teeth could be forgiven. I rushed home and told my mother.

"We're having a contest at school for the prettiest girl."

As usual, her head was in the oven. She wiped the perspiration off her forehead and stared at me.

"What does that have to do with you?"

"We are all going to walk in front of the school, then the other students vote."

My mother was taking out the freshly baked bread.

"That's the dumbest thing I've ever heard."

"Well, everyone has to do it and the teacher said, wear your prettiest dress."

I owned one school dress that everyone had already seen me wear. On school days I usually wore pleated skirts like most of the other girls. My dress was blue and white cotton, tiny checks, simple and plain. I had an idea.

"I'm going to ask Monica if I can borrow one of hers."

Monica, one of my Catholic cousins, had special dresses for church on Sunday. I borrowed a grey chemise dress from Monica. She was shorter than me, so I had to keep pulling the bottom hem over my boney knees. I put it on the morning of the school contest, walking on air and completely delusional. I watched Stephanie arrive with her father as usual. When he emerged from the car, he opened the back door and brought out a large garment bag. Stephanie skipped alongside her father while he carried her bag into the classroom. Her father placed it carefully on her desk, and when the teacher arrived, Stephanie slowly unzipped the bag to reveal the most beautiful dress we'd ever laid our eyes on. It was light blue and had flounce after flounce of sheer nylon over a large crinoline. To top it off, Stephanie was sporting a matching tiara over her perfectly spaced ringlets.

I never had a chance. When it was my turn to walk past the other students, my gait was awkward. I heard giggling from some of the boys and was sure they were laughing at me. Who did I think I was fooling? I began to lower my expectations. Once again, this was proof that I had no chance to be like everyone else. The secrets I had to keep about my home life put a constant strain on me at school.

This house was where my little brother Patrick peed blood, and then disappeared from our lives forever. He was my favourite brother, quiet and reserved, his thick dark hair and green eyes a contrast to all the blonds in the family. He didn't live long enough to get his first report card. When I came home from the first day of school that year, I learned he was gone. He was so excited about starting grade one, and looked so handsome in his grey slacks, white shirt and green cardigan, that morning when he left for school. I was looking forward to hearing how his day had gone when I came home.

"Did Paddy like his first day at school?"

The kitchen was unusually empty, just my mother leaning against the counter smoking, and staring out the kitchen window. She just looked at me, not speaking for what felt like a long time.

"He's in the hospital, he came home early because he was pee-ing blood."

My mother's words were flat and matter-of-fact.

"What's wrong with him?"

There was no reply, and my mother quickly averted her eyes.

"Go get changed and come help me with dinner."

From that day on my mom rarely mentioned Paddy, our nickname for him, or how he was doing, and I could see the sadness in her eyes. When he went into the hospital, she told us that he had asked if he could get a pony when he came home. He was six years old, and I suppose a pony was every little boy's dream. I found out he was never coming home when I overheard her talking to my father one evening, their voices unusually hushed. That was one of the few times I heard my mother cry. Then she said to my father.

"Patrick told me today that he doesn't think he'll need that pony now, children have a sixth sense."

After five months in hospital he died of cancer, no explanation, and we never saw him again. The day after my mom told me the pony story, I arrived home from school to find my older cousin Beth and her current boyfriend waiting for me in their Chevy Impala, no explanation offered. We drove across town to the Children's Hospital, while Patrick was in a hospital on the other side of the city.

"Put this gown on and climb into bed."

A doctor was waiting when I arrived, but I was a wise ten-year-old, already reading between the lines of adult conversations.

"I'm not sick, why am I in the hospital?"

He turned to leave, and I called out to him.

"Did my brother die?"

I sat in the hospital for three days, no one came to visit, or talk to me about what was going on, other than to ask me, "Would you like lime, or strawberry Jello.

I was picked up with no warning a few days later, as mysteriously as I was dropped off.

"Get dressed, your parents are here to take you home."

There was no conversation as I slid into the back seat of the car, and they drove off. I stared out the window at people walking around, going about their daily lives. Finally, I found enough courage to speak.

"Did Paddy die?"

No one turned to look at me. Eventually, the words came through the back of my mother's head.

"We buried him yesterday, it's all over."

There were no more questions or tears because I knew better. When I was older and had children of my own, I could only imagine the pain she must have been in. I have one black-and-white photo of her sitting beside Paddy's hospital bed. She is looking down at him, his gaunt pale face is looking back. He died the following week.

Around this time there was a picture and story on the front page of, 'The Vancouver Sun.' A little girl my age, Carolyn Moore, had been murdered. For some reason I was obsessed with death. My dreams fluctuated between the joy of me flying over houses across the sky and a murdered child, Carolyn Moore. One night she appeared beside my bed. The small black and white photograph of her on the front page of the paper stayed in my memory for years.

"Please don't worry about me, I'm fine now," she told me, and the dreams ended.

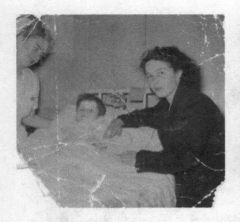

Childhood grocery store

Syl and Patrick in Hospital one month before he passed away.

Cousin Joan, Megan and Sister

Megan in Mayday celebration for Queen Elizabeth II

Megan with her grandmother Elizabeth
Hutton

CHAPTER SIX

Bouncing The Ball

Pop beads were in. It was 1954 and I was eight. Mine were covered with my teeth marks. Girls were not allowed to wear pants, and I spent half my recess and lunch hour trying to keep my skirt between my knees. I was learning valuable lessons about being a girl. What I looked like counted more than who I was, or how I felt. I could tell I was already running a deficit. My long blonde hair was fine and fly-away, my two front teeth protruded, and had a gap between them large enough for my tongue. I tried to be brave when the boys at school taunted me.

"Bucky beaver, hey you got any carrots for us."

And then chortle, chortle. I was already aware that I was not trying to impress the boys. I just looked at them like the morons they were proving to be. At home, my father told me to stand with the broom handle against my front teeth to push them back. I was learning that it didn't matter that I hated math, because my teacher only spent time with the boys. If I could make white sauce without lumps and sew an apron by grade eight, I would have it made. Secretly, I had rejected all of that, but I was wise enough to keep it to myself at least for the time being. My mother kept telling me.

"You need to change your attitude, or you'll never have friends."

My mother couldn't acknowledge that friends were not possible for me, while I lived at home with my unpredictable father. She warned me that if I didn't conform, my life could be difficult. I wasn't born to be a conformer.

"You can't always buck the system, sometimes you need to give in."

Chewing on my pop beads quelled my anxiety, I said to myself, no way.

I was already finding life interesting and slowly figuring out how to navigate with the least amount of collateral damage. I had been pegged as difficult, even as a young child I was outspoken when it suited me. I looked around, and decided I liked me just the way I was. I was already easily bored. I learned that I needed to be careful with boys because I didn't want to give them the wrong idea. It would take me a while to figure that one out. The wrong idea about what? I was pretty sure it had something to do with the whispers the adults didn't think I heard.

"You will need to watch that one."

Apparently, blonde hair was a sign of caution in those days.

The adults gave me nicknames, I remember from the age of three. Blondie, or the blonde bomber, are ones I remember well. I remember getting upset at the teasing, then being told, 'Be a good sport.' I didn't realize the power of being born blonde until much later.

My aunts were fearful that I would lead their daughters astray. My closest Catholic cousin spent an inordinate amount of time in confession, without my influence.

" I was only thinking those things, I wasn't going to do them,"

She would protest, heading for the confessional, just in case.

And there was me, content to throw my red, white, and blue, rubber ball against the cement wall, a meditative trance at recess, the repetitive bounce, challenging my reaction time. Me against myself. Throw, bounce, catch. Observing my peers from the sidelines was less complicated than trying to join them. I learned early, there is safety in solitude, a state of being, void of entanglement and judgment. Most of the time, I was confident and tenacious, self-contained and motivated, much to my mother's chagrin.

My mother was different that way, she wanted to please everyone, but I was discerning and thought she was wrong. I wasn't born to please. I was born to survive.

After my six-year-old brother Patrick died of cancer, I knew for sure that I would die too one day. Up until then, I made deals with the almighty and said my prayers faithfully. I thought about the Queen and wondered if she would ever die? My uncle Bill had given my mother a beautiful gold-embossed coronation book when Queen Elizabeth was crowned in June of 1953. I was allowed to look at it if promised not to stick my fingers in my mouth to turn the pages. I was enthralled with the coloured photographs. Queen Elizabeth's crowns, her dollhouse, the charmed life of a princess and a queen. I was convinced if I'd been born a queen, or at the very least a princess, I would live forever. Once Patrick died, I knew I was mortal. Years later, my mother showed me the lifeless body of her perfectly formed aborted fetus.

"I don't know what to do with it."

She looked at me as though I might have an answer. The simplicity of my bouncing ball came to mind. Throw, bounce, catch. A meditative trance that required no questions and no answers.

CHAPTER SEVEN

Symbols

To this day I believe what my mother told me.

"Your uncle was eaten by the fish in the Fraser River."

All the events around that time stuck with me. It was the first death I was to experience through my mother's eyes. Her twin brother in a boating accident, and missing for three months, found and identified by a wallet. In my ten-year-old mind, I wondered where the wallet had been? Didn't the fish eat his pants? How much of my uncle did they actually eat?

I couldn't ask my mother those questions. The most vivid visual memory is my mother holding up a one-dollar bill that was in my uncle's wallet.

I looked for signs of mystery in that money, but all I could see was a dollar bill, much like any other. It eventually went the way of all one-dollar bills. It was used for a loaf of bread.

"A dollar's a dollar," my mother said, when she sent me to the store.

That was the summer I discovered women. Mila Spencer to be exact. She lived in a big white house, surrounded by shrubs, and a three-foot cedar fence. The fence didn't serve any purpose. It just surrounded the house and brought attention to the much-needed paint job.   Mila was about fifteen, and I had my eye on her, every waking moment. I kept a picture of her, cut up of course, as all my pictures are from the fifties.

Mila, standing staring down at the ground, one foot slightly ahead of the other, a gaping hole where the person she was talking to, once stood.

That was my process of eliminating unwanted forces back then. A sharp pair of scissors and click, click, gone, at least from sight. Mila with her almost white, blonde hair bobbed around her face, wearing a plain white blouse, pleated skirt, and white and black saddle shoes.

Every Friday night Mila's parents went out, and I got to see Mila's breasts, because my bedroom window looked straight into Mila's kitchen. I don't know why she would choose the kitchen to make out with her boy friend but there they were every Friday night, without fail. I would get the dishes done in record time, and head off to my room, "to read." Then I would sit back and wait.

It was always the same. First Mila would unbutton her blouse, looking up at the sex crazed boy waiting so patiently to get at her, not to mention me, staring entranced through the slit in my closed bedroom curtains. When all the buttons were undone, Mila's breasts would be looking out at me, although still covered by a stark white bra.

Only then would the mystery begin. Mila would lean against the kitchen table and the boy would put his arms around her waist, gradually moving them higher, until his hands covered her breasts, I so patiently waited for Mila to uncover.

Next thing I knew the bra would be lying on the table and Mila's arms would be wrapped around the boys back as he went methodically from one side to another. I had no idea why he was doing it, or how it was for Mila, or the boy at that time. I just knew I wanted to do whatever it was that he did, and I wanted to do it with Mila.

The week that my uncle was found "half eaten by the fish" turned out to be a lucky one for me. I felt bad for my uncle, of course, and for my mother. She didn't cry often, and when she did, the little bit of security I had, was threatened. Showing emotion was not a positive thing in my house.

Mila was to spend the night, while my father drove my mother to a relative's house. From there she would catch the Greyhound bus and go up north to her brother's funeral.

As luck would have it, I wasn't my father's favorite, nor my mother's, and I would be staying home. My younger sister, who shared my bed, was going to keep my mother company. It worked out just the way I would have planned it. Mila and me, alone at last, although we weren't alone. The boys were scattered throughout the house in various rooms. They were there, but not a direct interference to the plan I had in my mind for Mila.

Mila arrived and I turned coy. She was our baby-sitter and didn't know I was in love with her. My past record for attracting attention wasn't very good. To be perfectly blunt, I was every baby-sitter's nightmare. A brat. My experience with attention was limited. If I was good, no one noticed me. If I wasn't, everyone did. I elicited negative attention everywhere. My insular world was vast, and I experimented with reaction, like a professional con artist. I had about twelve hours to convince Mila that she needed me.

When peace reigned and Mila sat down in front of the television, I made my move.

"Are you tired?"

I stretched my skinny shapeless ten-year-old frame in an exaggerated manner, my mouth open wide, head flung back, and my torso contorting in a ridiculous angle, and then answered myself, "I am."

Mila was in a state of hormonal flux, and I think she knew I had something on my mind. It had already been discussed that she would sleep in my room, if of course that was fine with her. I appeared to have more appeal than Ed Sullivan with his stiff neck, and eyes that stayed riveted to one area. The acrobats were just beginning to form a complete "V" when Mila got up and froze them in that position.

I was already in my flannelette pyjamas. I didn't have enough sense back then to be embarrassed by the Dalmatians, cavorting about my pant legs. I didn't know anything about seduction, or did I?

Mila wasn't sure how to undress in front of me. She pulled off her sweater. I can still see it, pink angora, with a white cotton collar. The sweater had short sleeves, and tiny little holes which were patterns of flowers. They wound endlessly across the front of the bodice, just low enough for Mila's bra to show, if she moved the right way. Mila held the pink fluffy sweater over her bra as she struggled with the back fastener. This wasn't going well.

Mila wasn't showing the confidence I had seen on her face as she unbuttoned her blouse for that boy I cut out of the picture. I scrambled onto the bed, jumping under the covers. I giggled and pulled my legs up. I made a tent, and surveyed my territory, excited beyond my own comprehension. Mila finally crawled into my bed.

Not one word was uttered. She was smooth, Mila was, and stark naked. My breathing stopped, and I remember thinking, now what? It looked so easy watching Mila's face turned up towards the ceiling, her lovely wide mouth open, while her eyes fluttered and closed, when that boy did things to her in the kitchen.

Where did I go from here, my hands were cold and I put them together for a moment, then stuck them between my knees. My leg touched Mila's thigh, and she turned towards me. I was warm all over. I knew at that moment, I was not what my family made me out to be, a girl who would chase the boys. Long Blonde hair, my curse, blonde bomber, blondie, these names all held negative connotations for me. Even as a five-year-old as I sat in the tub and watched my hair swirl around my belly button, I knew. That was the day my mother walked in, and caught me staring off into space. It was something I did often which worried her.

"Are you ready to get out?" she asked.

Instead of answering, I continued to stare at the wall, and stated firmly,

"When I grow up, I'm going to love women."

Mila's hand was touching my hair. The tips of her fingers lightly fell on my forehead as she lifted strands and pulled them between her fingers. My head was on fire, such a small gesture but packed with erotic overtones. At ten, erotic was often confused with other words, and I had no knowledge of the feelings raging through me.

It can take a long time for one body to move towards another, or it can happen in an instant. This was not going anywhere fast. Mila continued to pull long strands of my hair through her fingers, and I continued to lie there, my eyes closed. I thought about starting a conversation, but what would I say. I spoke anyway. What I did say was stupid, not at all well thought out, just like everything else I did back then.

"Does your mom know that boy comes over on Friday night?"

Mila's hand caught my long blonde locks, and accidentally pulled them.

"Ouch!"

"Sorry," she pulled the covers up to her chin and stared at the ceiling.

"What are you talking about?"

"That boy, you know, THAT boy." I was losing my nerve. Mila didn't sound happy, and the warm feeling I felt in my body a few minutes earlier was turning to chills.

We were at an impasse. I yawned loudly and closed my eyes praying for a miracle to come my way. At that moment, Mila pulled me to her.

It was a closed coffin, but a beautiful funeral my mother said. Everyone was impressed with my little sister's perfect behavior, and she made a direct hit with the aunts and uncles. I as usual, wanted all the grim details.

Did the fish really eat him? Which part did they eat? Did they eat his face? It repulsed me and intrigued me at the same time. My mother was upset because someone had taken the banner which read "brother" off the coffin and kept it. My mother thought she should have it, because he was her twin. With my ten-year-old wisdom I agreed, but already I was thinking about Mila. Not long after all these events, Mila moved away. The following Friday, I went to my room only to find her kitchen curtains closed. It was months before I got over the trauma. My mother eventually stopped talking about her brother and months later I heard her telling a neighbor.

"The banner was just a symbol, I had him, he was my twin."

Then she said, "No one can take that away." The neighbor, then commented that she should get the clothes off the line, before those clouds rolled in.

I ran into Mila again only once, "I know you!"

I didn't learn to mull my thoughts over before I spoke, until well into my thirties. I, of course had changed a lot, she, little. Then I remembered Mila's breasts. She was standing with two boys, men now, looking at me. I recognized one as the space beside Mila in the picture.

Then my brain moved ahead of my tongue. "Maybe I don't."

Mila's photograph lies in a box amidst old report cards, and brownie pins. Every five years or so, when I sort, I mean to throw away those things, but I don't.

I guess, somehow, something that was once so important, has become a symbol. And, in my way of remembering, it is all tied together. Dead uncles, fish, banners which read, "brother," and things people can never take away, like my night with Mila.

CHAPTER EIGHT

Up In Smoke

Once again with little notice, my dad decided he was moving us.

"Your dad and I are going to look at a dairy farm tomorrow."

My mom rarely went anywhere with him, other than to the grocery store.

"Are we moving?"

I was ten and a half and had almost made a friend at school, my favourite cousins lived nearby. In one year, we'd buried my brother, my grandfather and my mother's twin brother. We'd moved to bigger houses before, but this time we were leaving Patrick behind and alone, in the cemetery on Fraser Street.

"We'll see, that's what he says."

I knew my mother had no control over any of the decisions, big or small.

Before school began in the fall we were on the dairy farm. My father sold our Vancouver house, and our new home was in the country, about three miles from my new school. There was nothing in sight, other than smaller farms spaced out over the land. An old wooden United Church stood on the corner beside one small grocery store. The farm gave us space, and because he wasn't home as early, we had a bit more freedom. We could be outside playing games we'd make up, or in the barn, sliding from the top into the hay.

With so many young children around, there were unexpected events and tragedies. One day, my brother left a bucket of boiling water he was taking to the barn on the kitchen floor. He was much too young and small to be allotted that task, but like all of us, he had little choice. Our baby brother, who was about 10 months old, crawled over and tipped the bucket all over himself.

He was wearing a green wool sweater my mother had knit for him, and the boiling water made the wool stick to his skin. I remember him standing screaming in his crib before he was taken to the hospital. He had third-degree burns all over his chest and was in the hospital for a long time. I was becoming immune to death, loss and tragedy.

My parents always sent us to Sunday school; it didn't matter what the affiliation was if it wasn't Catholic. My father was the only one in his family who was not a practicing Catholic, and we were disparaged by his relatives. My cousins all went to Catholic schools. To most of his family, we were heathens. My mother expressed her opinion about this situation over and over.

"They're just a bunch of bloody hypocrites, and think they're better than the rest of us, how Christian is that?"

My mother, coming from the Presbyterian backwoods, had a lifelong disdain for Catholics, except my grandmother. My Irish grandmother was warm-hearted and down-to-earth, and she expressed little respect for her adult children, who treated us as religious outcasts.

Because the church was an escape from home, I embraced it with a vengeance. The United Church was where I pledged my allegiance to God and the Queen, every Thursday after school. Wearing my navy skirt, and white middy with the sailor collar, I became a CGIT, a Canadian Girl in Training. Then on Sundays, I'd stand in front of the congregation at the Evangelical Free

Church, and sing solos: 'I Went to the Garden Alone.' or, with more gusto, 'How Great Thou Art.' My life was a lie. I couldn't connect with any of my schoolmates except on a superficial level. I lived permanently with the fear of my secret being discovered, that my father was a simmering lunatic who ruled our home with his iron fist. Having friends was out of the question because having friends meant bringing them home to your house, at least occasionally. Instead, I learned to improvise and tried to fit in on the edge of things as much as possible.

My new school wasn't a smooth transition. Most of my peers had grown up in the area and were a close-knit group. It was a small-town school, and no one was looking for new friendships. I thought there was a chance when a grade six ball team started up in the mornings before school. Heather, the older girl who ran the team, was the school bully, and everyone was afraid of her. I wasn't, and I wanted to fit in. She ran everything.

The new rule is, the first players to get here and touch the base get to play. I went home exhilarated and told my mom.

"I need to leave early tomorrow because I want to play ball."

The next morning, I rushed out of the house. I ran and ran, until I had to stop and catch my breath, then ran again. I remember the panic I felt at the thought of not making it in time. When I arrived, there was no one else in the schoolyard. I touched the plate, then flopped down on the grass. Before long, Heather showed up. She glared at me.

"What are you doing here?"

"I ran all the way here so I could be sure to play."

She stared me down, which was a feat. There wasn't much I was afraid of anymore.

"Well, you can't play."

She tossed her bat behind home plate.

"But you said...and I touched the plate."

"I make up the rules here."

I tried not to let my devastation show. Inside, I was crying for acceptance at my new school.

"I don't like you and you can't play."

So much for fitting in. I was learning that I couldn't trust anyone. Letting my guard down hadn't been easy, and I began to build new walls around every part of me. Apart from church, the one other thing I loved was the time I could spend with my younger siblings, bringing in the hay, collecting eggs, and feeding the cows. A swing set in the front yard provided hours of enjoyment. I made up games to keep them occupied, taking turns to see who could jump the furthest off the swing. I was beginning to relax into my adolescence.

My father's moods and violent outbursts were constant. The belt had been upgraded to a bull whip also known as a "Cat' O Nine Tails." It was a thick long lash of braided leather with loose thongs at the bottom that wrapped painfully around arms or legs. I'd become proficient at staying out of my father's way, but my younger brothers weren't so lucky. One was always targeted, and I would cover my ears trying to shut out his screams. My mother would look sad and sometimes try to stop him.

Our second summer on the farm, what began as a blue-sky day turned ugly. My cousins were visiting with my Aunt Mary, my dad's only sister, a psychiatric nurse, warm and kind, and like my grandmother, no-nonsense. My father was usually on his best behaviour as long as possible around her. When we had lived nearby in Vancouver, these family gatherings happened more often, but once we moved and my father got crazier, we were more distant from his family.

I could see that Aunt Mary tolerated him, but also that she felt sorry for my mother.

I'd spent a rare day letting my body relax, feeling the sun on my face, and laughing with my cousins. We tricked our city cousins into touching the electric fence, and we watched baby mice burrow between the bales of hay in the fields. I remember thinking that maybe there would be more times like this. I felt like a carefree child, an unfamiliar feeling.

We ended that glorious day with a small bonfire beside our house and a marshmallow roast. I thought that someone had heard my prayers, and the tide was turning. I rarely spoke to my father for any reason, and I can't remember in my entire childhood ever saying the word 'Dad.' This day felt safe, and as it was ending, I risked asking if I could toast another marshmallow. My back was turned when I felt his steel-toed boot between my legs, the pain so instant and severe I thought I would die. I limped to my room alone and writhed on my bed, the pain searing through my small body. I was afraid he had damaged me so that I would never be able to have my own children.

A month later, I survived another year, and was going into Junior High at a new school.

"Do you think I can get my hair cut before school starts?"

My mom believed that girls should have long hair, so I was surprised at her prompt reply. Although I knew her beliefs weren't based on religion, it was as though long hair on girls was sacred. She answered me almost too quickly, and I was surprised and relieved.

"I know someone who does it out of her house, I'll see if she can take you." The following day my long hair was transformed into a loose curled bob, just above my shoulders. I couldn't stop looking at it in the mirror, enchanted, but the following morning it was a frizzy mess. School was starting the next day, so my mother decided she'd fix it. She twisted pink foam rollers all over my head. The frizz turned into dozens of tight tiny ringlets; my fine hair was not letting them go. I had to catch the school bus and was about to start my first day of

Grade Eight looks like a cross between Shirley Temple and a wolfhound. There was no way I could go to my class. I stayed in the locker room when the bell rang, sitting on the floor, with no idea what my next move would be. On my first day of Junior High, the last thing I wanted was to stand out. Before long, Mr. Cudworth, my new home-room teacher, appeared.

"Hey, I wondered what happened to you, when I did roll call, you were missing, is anything wrong?"

Mr. Cudworth became my first favourite teacher.

"Look at my hair, I can't go to class like this."

It was everywhere. Some of the ringlets were intact, while others had turned into a bird's nest from me trying to brush them straight.

"You go into the washroom and see what you can do to fix it, then come to the class." Much later in the year, a classmate told me that Mr. Cudworth had come back to the classroom and warned everyone, that if anyone laughed at me or made comments, they would all get a detention.

I would be friendless in Junior High; my standards for friends were high. I was accustomed to my own company by now, and I had my writing and my books. A teenage girl who wasn't chasing boys and trying to lose her virginity wasn't very exciting. While other girls my age worried about what they looked like and how popular they were, I wrote poetry. I was already labelled weird and beginning the year with a hair disaster was just the icing on the cake.

Everyone remembered.

"You're that girl who sat in the locker room crying, aren't you?"

Sharon became the mean girl replacing Heather from my last school. Sharon could smell my fear, and her eyes would narrow into tiny slits. One morning she caught me at my locker.

"Hey, you've got nothing there, flat as a pancake."

She grabbed the back of my sweater and held it taut across my flat chest.

Humiliated in front of my classmates, I watched her walk away, full of mean confidence, her tight black pencil skirt showing off her firm ass.

Sharon had it in for me all year, taking every opportunity to bully me.

I'm not sure why I didn't stand up to her. I just wanted to fly under the radar as low as possible, but she kept calling attention to my presence. A few months passed, and I finally bucked up.

On a Sunday night before the start of a new week, I decided that come hell or high water, I was going to school with breasts. I went into my mother's top drawer and borrowed her bra and a pair of nylon stockings. I knew my mother wouldn't miss them because she only dressed up for funerals, and no one had died recently. During the day, she always wore jeans and a baggy plaid shirt. She always had a pocket for her cigarettes. If she was going out to buy groceries with my dad, she'd press a pair of slacks and wear a nice, flowered blouse. A couple of weeks before, I had borrowed her garter belt and wore her nylon stockings to school. When I stood up to change classes, the belt fell to my knees. My body was skinny and shapeless, and I had no hips to hold it up. I struggled with the bra and carefully stuffed the stockings into each cup, making sure they were even. I checked myself out carefully in the bathroom mirror on the medicine chest. When I arrived at school, Sharon was hovering around the locker room as usual. I removed my coat carefully so I wouldn't disturb anything. Sharon noticed immediately.

"Titties, wow, you're finally catching up to the rest of us."

I spent the remainder of the day preoccupied with trying to keep them in place. When I moved, they shifted, one larger than the other. I kept my elbows close to my chest so I could move them back into place, hopefully unnoticed.

At home, my mother still worked from morning to night. By this time, we were seven children, eight, if you counted my brother Patrick, lying alone in the cemetery on Fraser Street, back in Vancouver. Christmas was approaching and my mother made another announcement one night.

"Your dad and I are going to look at some places up north on the weekend, he wants to buy a ranch."

The dairy farm appeared to whet my father's appetite for acquiring something on a larger scale. We had no idea what, "up north," meant. The dairy farm had cows I'd grown to love. They all had names above their stalls, like Bambi and Star. They were gentle Jerseys, Guernseys and hardy Holsteins. I loved their large eyes and their soft mooing sounds. My brothers were in charge of the milking, done with Surge milking machines which were then placed outside the large metal gate to be picked up by the dairy.

Now we were moving away. When I was eight, we left the house our grandfather bought for us because we needed more room. I was ten at the next house where my brother peed blood and died. I made one friend there, Sheilah, and I named my baby sister after her. I went into grade four at that house, chewed on my pop beads, and bounced my rubber ball on the cement wall at recess.

"I don't want to move again."

My mother was filling a cigarette paper with tobacco and licking it.

"Well, we have no choice, take care of the little kids, and don't burn the house down." They rolled back into the driveway on Sunday night. My mother appeared dazed by the sudden decision to uproot us again. Dazed, but also, there was an excitement about it for her. Growing up in an isolated community, she loved the bush and the outdoors.

"We looked at three places, and your dad put an offer on one."

"So, when are we moving?"

By now, I knew life was never predictable.

"The one he wants is over seven hundred acres, lots of trees, a pond and a small waterfall behind the house on the mountain."

She made it sound as if we were going on a vacation, something we had never done.

"Where is it?"

I just knew that it was a long way from everything I knew.

"Up north, about five hundred miles from here, it'll probably take us about eight or nine hours to drive up there with all you kids."

"When are we leaving?"

"After Christmas."

Barely thirteen, I was leaving everything behind again, the house where I had to run past the graveyard, the white church on the corner where I pledged allegiance to the flag every Thursday night.

I was leaving the church where I sang solos in front of the congregation and praised a Lord, I wasn't sure existed. It was late December when we drove away, my brother, without a licence, driving the U-Haul with everything we owned. The Fraser Canyon Highway was rugged, the road carved into the steep mountains. I tried to ignore the fast-moving waters below us. We passed through whistle stops with names like Horsefly, Boston Bar, and Spuzzum.

When we were hungry our father gave us bread and cheese. I was scrunched in the front seat of the Grey Plymouth between my father and my mother, relegated to that spot because I was prone to car sickness.

"The last thing I need is you throwing up all over the kids in the back seat."

Sitting that close to my father made me even more anxious, and I knew it would be a long ride.

My friend at the Evangelical Free Church, Ruth, had gifted me with a Blue Bible in a small Cedar box. Whenever I felt like crying, I'd open the box so I could smell the Cedar. I was going to miss Ruth and her kindness, but not the services and all the Pastor's dire warnings.

"There will come a time, my friend, if you've not yet given your life to the Lord Jesus Christ if you've not taken Him as your Saviour."

I experienced enough dire warnings at home, I didn't need them from him too. The Lord had little to do with me wanting to be there, I could see right through the Pastor's words. I knew that small children were taken even if they hadn't done anything to deserve dying.

My father's leisurely driving didn't match his moods. My mother was in a hurry to get there.

"For Christ's sake, can't you go any faster?"

He didn't turn his head to acknowledge my mother, who was chewing on her bottom lip.

"We're never going to get there at this rate."

She probably needed to have a smoke, and he wouldn't have stopped for that.

"Mind your own business, I'm driving, not you."

We drove by ancient cemeteries at the side of the roads, weathered wooden crosses leaning sideways like forgotten soldiers. They made me think of Paddy again, the picture I had in my mind, of his grave: a white harp of flowers my grandma had placed there, a stark contrast to the mound of black dirt, his name, Paddy, written across the front on a large ribbon. In death, more attention than he probably got during his short life.

We were moving from a moderate West Coast climate to a Northern one. Before we left, my mother ordered everyone new winter coats from the Sears catalogue. She always managed to dress us well from her family allowance and charge accounts from Sears and Eaton's. I was to learn very quickly, what "up north," meant. My hair and eyelashes would freeze on the way to the school bus. Our new home began at a long driveway with a big metal gate and a cattle guard. The house stood in the distance on a knoll, at the base of a small mountain. Behind the house over the small mountain, there was a waterfall.

It would have been idyllic if we weren't isolated with the father we feared. There was no consideration for anyone's needs but his, he always came first. If he wanted to buy cattle, he bought them; if my mother needed anything for the children, she had to scrimp and save from her family allowance.

The high school was about thirty miles away, and we walked to the school bus. The bus stop was at the main highway; decades later I went back and clocked the walk. It was over six miles.

Apart from our house on the hill and the one just below our gate, there were no other houses until we reached the highway. Every morning we walked down the deserted dirt road hoping that the wildlife lurking in the bushes behind the barbed wire fences would stay there. We often spotted deer, foxes, coyotes and the occasional wolf. We weren't afraid of those animals. It was the black bears we feared. As usual, our father had the solution.

"If you come across a bear, don't try to outrun it, just play dead."

I was terrified. I was old enough now to understand what a bear could do to me. Unlike my mother, there was no Annie Oakley in me. One morning on my way to the bus, I fell. I was stumbling along, trying to remove my rollers from my hair before I made it to the bus stop. The road was rough and filled with ruts, and I slipped on a patch of ice, the pain in my kneecap excruciating. I bit my lip all the way to school. The school nurse looked at my knee and took me to the hospital. I'd torn my cartilage, limping for the next few months.

We inherited a Clydesdale horse with our house. Tess was very old, gentle and big enough for two of us to sit on at once. She didn't move very quickly but was perfect for kids who knew nothing about horses. The first winter we were riding her when she slipped on the ice and fell. My father came outside. He looked at Tess struggling to get up.

"A lame horse is no good to anyone."

He went inside, came back with a shotgun and shot her in front of us. We were horrified but said nothing.

My sister and I invented some interesting games to keep us entertained on the ranch when he wasn't around. A large Brahma bull lived in an enclosure near the main barn. My sister and I invented our own, 'Running with the Bull,' game. She was three years younger and could already outrun me.

"You climb on the fence and when I give you the signal, run to the other side of the pen." I distracted the bull, while she jumped off the fence and sprinted across the enclosure, scrambling onto the other side.

"Run, run, hurry up, he's turning around," I'd yell at her."

He wore a loud clanging bell so we could hear when he began to move. We'd be panting and breathless, proud of ourselves for avoiding his sharp horns one more time.

My mother was happier in this isolated place than I'd seen her in a long time, perhaps ever. One day she was peering out the window towards the pond about fifty feet from our house. There was a large thicket adjacent to the pond where we often spotted deer. Suddenly, I heard her voice rise and saw a half-smile on her face.

"Jesus Christ, there's a moose down by the pond."

I never knew if she was taking the Lord's name in vain or asking the almighty for help. She grabbed her gun from the rack beside the door and ran towards the pond. I watched while she hoisted it to her shoulder and took aim. I hated the crack of a gun, but it was part of her childhood and she hunted whenever she could, well into her seventies. This occasion didn't go as expected. It was a cow moose with a young calf somewhere in the bushes. My mother just managed to graze it and make it angry. The moose charged while I watched in horror from the living room window. Thankfully my mother was a fast runner, the grazed moose not up to its usual speed. She fell through the back door out of breath.

"Jesus, did you see that, I had to run like a son of a bitch."

She was grinning and panting at the same time.

It was apparent from the beginning that, once again, no one was looking for friends at my new school. Most of the families had lived in the area for years and newcomers didn't become part of the community easily. The fact that I lived thirty miles out of town didn't help. A few weeks into my new school I was approached by a girl in my class.

"Hey, you wanna go for a ride with me and some friends after school?"

Her bleached blonde hair was held up by a stiff hairband, and she was chewing a large wad of bubble gum. I hesitated at first but quickly changed my mind.

"Sure, why not."

I'd never been in a car with strangers, and certainly not with teenagers. In five minutes, I knew I'd made a mistake. The blonde was singing along to "Lonely Boy," blaring from the car radio, popping her gum and bobbing her head.

The boy driving the car sped up during the chorus and joined her.

"I'm just a lonely boy, lonely and blue…"

They were driving too fast, and it was apparent I was out of my element, clutching the side of my car door.

"Hey just relax, have a swig of this, it'll help ya."

She pulled a bottle of vodka from her pink plastic purse and shoved it towards me. I'd never tasted alcohol.

"Up north" held a variety of surprises.

I tipped the bottle to my lips and took a quick gulp before I began to cough.

I was sure I was going to throw up all over the bleached blonde's pink purse.

"I need you to stop the car and let me out."

The blonde lit up a cigarette and was blowing smoke in my face, her eyes beginning to glaze over.

"Let her out, guys, before she pukes all over me."

The car screeched to a sudden halt, and I got out grateful to be alive. If these were the only friend openings, I wasn't interested.

A few weeks later a pain in my abdomen intensified to the point where I could barely sleep. I'd been suffering for a few weeks and finally mentioned it to my mother. Like all the pains in my life, I preferred keeping it to myself.

"It could be your appendix," she threw out that possibility."

This was a possibility, but not one anyone prepared to act on. She didn't drive and the town was 30 miles away. A couple of days later, I collapsed at school while walking up the stairs to change classes. I arrived by ambulance at the local hospital where a gruff older doctor examined me.

"What do you think is wrong?"

He was impatient, rough and unfriendly.

"It could be my appendix."

I was repeating my mother's words.

"Oh, so now you're a doctor, are you, well if you think it's your appendix let's take it out."

I felt powerless. I don't remember my parents coming to the hospital before or after the surgery. I woke up the next day with my abdomen bandaged from under my breasts to the top of my pubic bone. The doctor had made a cut about twelve inches long, two inches to the right of my navel. When they removed the bandages, the area was infected. The nurses placed a large heat lamp beside my bed aimed at the wound. I was unable to move away from the heat and the lamp burned my incision. It left burns and blisters over the raw wound, eventually leaving me with a wide raised scar. Later in life it caused adhesions with other organs.

My outside scar now matched my inner ones. And it was all for nothing because it wasn't my appendix at all, it was an impacted bowel. My father controlled the length of time we were allowed in the bathroom too.

"Get the hell out, you've been in there long enough."

The ranch was the place where my brother learned that the lunatic wasn't his real father. He'd just turned sixteen and wanted to apply for his driver's licence. My mother looked uncomfortable when she spilled her secret for the first time.

"I have something to tell you, he's not your father."

She removed a worn photograph from her wallet. An attractive young woman with dark hair standing beside a handsome young man with a head full of blond curls, the same curls my brother had when he was a small boy.

"This is your father."

She ran her finger over his face in the photo as though touching it would bring him back.

"We were in love, and when the war broke out, he had to go overseas, we planned to get married when he returned, we wrote letters all through the war. He met you once when he came home on leave, a goddamn social worker found out I wasn't married, and threatened to take you away from me...."

Her voice trailed off and she was visibly upset, reliving the pain and loss.

"Anyway, he was your father, you have his hair and eyes, I don't know what happened and why he didn't come back, her voice trailed off."

My brother was upset when he heard the news. Not because the lunatic wasn't his father, but because somewhere out there was his real father. I in turn, was devastated that my whole brother, someone I looked up to, was reduced to a half in a matter of seconds. My mother lit a cigarette while my brother stared at the picture of his real father. Then she quickly grabbed the photograph and put it back into her wallet, where it would remain until her death, almost six decades later.

"Up north," held pleasant surprises too. There was the healthy organic food we regularly ate, our own meat, fruit and vegetables and my mother's home-baked bread. I remember the nights we played hockey with the German boys who lived at the bottom of our property. After dinner, we trudged down our long driveway to their frozen pond, skates over our shoulders. We played until our fingers and toes had lost all feeling. Walking back to our house, the sky would be lit up by thousands of stars, the only sound the clink of our skate blades, and the crunch of frozen snow under our feet.

In the end, it all came back to my father. Along with his need to control was his obsession with cleanliness.

There was never anything out of place or he would lose his mind. He searched for things to complain about. One night after dinner, my sister and I had finished the dishes and I was doing homework at the kitchen table. My father appeared out of nowhere and went into a rage. Apparently one of the frying pans wasn't cleaned to his liking.

"What do they teach you in school, to not do the dishes properly?"

He grabbed my textbooks and schoolwork and threw them into the cookstove. I sat frozen, watching and hearing a crucial part of my life go up in flames. There were no words, just the numb feeling that nothing was going to change if I lived in his house. My brother had recently moved out, and perhaps that had reminded my father that he was not my mother's first choice.

It wasn't long before his next violent rage. No one ever knew what would set him off. The small children were terrified and huddled on the staircase. I remember feeling helpless but wanting to protect them. My parents were yelling, and I was trying to keep everyone out of his path. Suddenly, he grabbed a shotgun from the rack and was waving it around.

"How about I just shoot all of you!"

There was pandemonium, my mother was shouting.

"For Christ sakes, put that gun down you lunatic."

My younger siblings were screaming and scrambling, their eyes wide with fear.

"Are we going to die?"

My mother was trying to wrestle the gun from him, and I wondered who was going to get shot first. Nothing surprised me anymore, but I knew this was my breaking point. I could no longer live with the pretence that I could save or protect anyone from my father. I was

exhausted. That was the official end of my childhood, and in many ways, my youth. From that night on I was about to experience a different kind of survival. I had just turned fourteen.

The following morning everyone was alive, my mother acting as though nothing had happened. She was baking bread, the wood in the stove was popping, and my sisters were getting ready for school. I had quietly packed a small bag the night before.

"Mom, I'm leaving, I'm going back to the coast."

She was staring out the window, the sadness and epiphany that she was powerless to change our situation written on her face.

"You're only fourteen."

In years yes, but I felt as though I'd lived a long time.

"I can't stay here with him anymore, don't worry about me, I can take care of myself." She grabbed a rolled cigarette and there was silence between us as she flicked her lighter and took a drag. I was holding back tears, I loved my mother, but knew that I couldn't live like this. She must have known it too, although neither of us wanted to say so out loud. All she could offer me were a few words of caution.

"Be careful."

I had little fear about outside forces, after living with such danger inside my home for so many years. She handed me a two-dollar bill.

"I wish I could give you more but he's such a cheap son of a bitch."

I felt guilty about taking it from her. It was no doubt her cigarette, or Kotex money for the month. Once when I was younger, I heard her ask him for money to buy menstrual pads, and she looked sheepish when he replied.

"What do you mean, I thought you had that already this month."

We hugged goodbye and her last words were:

"Take care of yourself and write when you get a place."

Our letters became our first real form of communication. I was able to say things to my mother that I couldn't when I lived with her. Through our letters I learned how much she cared about me. I left that morning, the tears flowing down my face known only to me.

I walked the six miles and a bit to the main highway. There were always families at the campground. I stood and watched a young couple with their two children before I approached them.

"I'm looking for a ride to Vancouver, I'm going to visit my grandmother."

They didn't hesitate. This was a different time, and it wasn't unusual to hitch rides if you lived in the country. When I reached the home of my uncle, my father's youngest brother, he didn't invite me in, or ask why I was there on my own. I walked to my grandmother's house about an hour away. She was furious at her son's cold shoulder to me.

"What's wrong with him, couldn't he even give you bus fare?"

She made me tea, and we ate a sandwich together while I made up a positive story to explain my sudden appearance. I loved her dearly but didn't want to burden her with my problems.

CHAPTER NINE

Breaking Free

Eventually, I reconnected with my Evangelical church and slept wherever I could get a bed, sometimes on the beach. The west coast rain came, and it was relentless. I was tired, often hungry and always lonely; it wore me down, physically and emotionally. But I loved my freedom and not having to hold my breath. On occasion my mom would send me small gifts, once a transistor radio. I'd take them to a pawn shop to get money to eat, often to the greyhound bus depot, or the White Lunch, on Hastings Street, where the homeless men hung out.

As I crossed a street one rainy day, a car narrowly missed hitting me, but in jumping out of the way, I fell. A bystander saw the incident and insisted on taking me to a hospital. I was unscathed from the fall but was diagnosed with a serious case of pneumonia. The doctors and nurses spent the next two weeks trying to get information from me.

"You need to tell us who you are, and where you live, your parents must be frantic, you're too young to be out here on your own."

There was no way to explain my life to them. I refused to tell them my name, or where I came from, because I was determined not to return to the ranch. Eventually they began playing hard ball.

"If you don't tell us your name and give us the contacts your family, we will have to put you in the juvenile detention home when you leave the hospital, we have no choice."

Why couldn't one of the nurses just take me home to a life without fear, where I would have a warm bed every night? At the end of their rope with me they brought in the big guns, the police. Soon I was on a plane with a female RCMP officer, returning to the hell I'd left. All the way back I told her defiantly.

"I didn't run away, I left, no one stopped me, you're wasting your time because I will leave again."

I suppose I was as incorrigible at that time, as I was tenacious. I felt trapped by circumstance. Day-to-day living was barely worth the effort. After my father tossed my books and schoolwork into the fire, I lost hope. My mother's past was catching up with me, the resignation she carried, living a life very different from her youthful dreams. It lay heavily on me, and it seemed there was no easy solution for either of us.

I was back at my old school, and I was living in the dorm with a matron and ten other girls, who lived too far away for a daily commute. I had no real experience with connection, I kept to myself. Those were still the days of secrets, keeping our private lives to ourselves. I wrote poetry in math class, instead of doing my work. The teachers had already given up on me. A poem I read in elementary school, The House with Nobody In It, gave me the urge to write poetry as a child. Poetry was my true friend. A simple poem about an empty house influenced me early to express myself with my words.

"So whenever I go to Suffern

Along the Erie track

I never go by the empty house

Without stopping and looking back."

For some reason it was a poem that resonated with me, and I could never get it out of my mind. It made me aware of the power of words to evoke feelings. Houses fascinated me.

Who lived in them, and what were their lives like? What was it like inside someone else's life?

I found an abandoned chipmunk outside and took it to my room. I made a home for it in my desk. I kept it for a few days, taking it out, and stroking its soft fur. Then I put it back outside, hoping a cat wouldn't get it.

Most weekends I stayed in the dorm on my own when the other girls were picked up by their parents. My dad wouldn't have wasted gas money coming to pick me up. Summer holidays were approaching, and the dorm would be closed. The students were sent home until the fall. I made an appointment with the school counsellor because I didn't plan to go back home. I would run away first. I was nervous and feeling desperate at the same time.

"Would you like to talk to someone?"

This would be the first time I opened the door a crack about my life at home. I had never hinted at the abuse. I was always afraid that if I spoke up to anyone my younger siblings could be taken away. My mother's children were all she had, the little bit of joy in her life.

My initial reaction was resistance and suspicion.

"My mom doesn't need any more trouble, she has enough with him."

She was attentive and I felt I could trust her with my story.

"I understand, and whatever you tell me is private."

I told her about my father, his violent outbursts and the unpredictabili-ty of my home life. She took some papers out of her desk and listened to me for a long time. I told her about the constant arguing, the bull-whip and the gun. She offered me a solution.

"I have an option that might work for you and take you away from here."

She opened her desk drawer and took out some papers.

"There is someone I'd like you to meet, he's a wonderful man, and I think the two of you would get along great."

A man and a stranger, my trust barometer was on zero.

"He comes up from the coast every month and visits local schools, if you want to meet him, you need to tell him everything you've told me, I'm sure he can help you."

I was regretting I'd opened my mouth. The shame I carried inside me because of my father almost overrode my need for safety.

"Think about it, Dr. Cashmore is a psychiatrist who works with young people, he has a large clinic on the coast."

"I don't need to see him, there is nothing wrong with me."

My mother's words were ringing in my ears.

At four, I had pleaded with my mother to leave, my awareness and ability to assess our situation at a young age was puzzling to her. I could see very clearly what she was too beaten down to admit. So many times, I pleaded with my mother.

"Why can't we go live somewhere far way where he can't find us?"

"We have nowhere to go, she would tell me, stay out of his way, and you'll be fine." When I expressed my feelings to my mom, she would look at me as if she had no idea where I came from. I could never forget the words she said to me when I was about four. I would wonder for years what the ending could be.

"I wonder if you're the way you are because…"

The way I was? A very aware child who could see how dysfunctional our lives were and powerless to do anything about it. Perception was my downfall, I learned early.

It would be decades before I understood what she meant, and why she couldn't finish the sentence. Throughout the years, when my feelings overwhelmed me, I often wondered if she was right, maybe there was something wrong with me. I didn't fit in here, did I fit in anywhere?

Sometimes nothing made sense. What did she mean?

Dr. Allan Cashmore and I began a wonderful, long relationship. As adults we became friends, and we stayed in touch for years. He came to my wedding and met my husband and our children.   He was my greatest support through the remainder of my teenage years. At my request we went to court. I was legally removed from my family, and I became a ward of the court. He found me a school in Vancouver, and a different life began. I felt a sense of freedom I'd never known before. I was astounded at how quiet life was outside my home. My body began to relax probably for the first time in my life. I wasn't waiting for the sky to fall. I felt as though I'd finally stopped running.

A new person had recently married into our family who gave me new hope. My father's brother Bill, or Uncle Willy, as we called him then, married my Aunt Martha later in life. She was so different from anyone I'd known, and the first time we met I felt a closeness I'd never experienced. I stayed with her for a few weeks during that tumultuous time when I moved back to Vancouver with the help of Dr.

Cashmore. Those days with her gave me renewed hope and energy for a future. She listened to my ramblings and appeared to understand a lonely teenaged girl. She told me about her own difficult childhood, her family, forced from their life in Russia, by the Revolution, home and business lost, and a complete start-over in Canada. Aunt Martha was affected by her mother's history, as I was by mine. That short place of refuge as a teenager, gave me an indication of what normal might feel like. We put on vinyl records, and I danced for my aunt in her living room. At night I went to sleep in peace. For the first time in my life, I felt there could be hope.

But I couldn't stay with Willie and Martha forever. In a short time, my aunt had given me the courage and the confidence to believe in myself, because she listened to me. Because of my maturity, I was allowed to live on my own in a variety of living situations. There were numerous apartment buildings and other shared living spaces at English Bay, in Vancouver. Young women from Australia and the UK often rented rooms for a few months or longer. Eventually, I began to believe in myself and knew there was nothing wrong with me. I had a controlling, unpredictable father and that wasn't my fault. In contrast to my own father, Dr. Cashmore and I would share tea over my latest poetry. He was like the father I wished I'd had. Dr. Cashmore and one of my English teachers, Olwyn Irving, saved me from complete despair, and gave me support through those difficult years. Decades later I'd written a play that was at the Fringe Festival in Vancouver. I looked Olwyn up because I'd mentioned her in my play. When we met after so many years, she made a comment that surprised me.

"You were such a vivacious young girl, and so full of life."

I was a damn good actress, that was all.

Life was a bit easier with these support systems, but I was young and on my own. Everyone had families. I was still adrift, and there were times when I almost gave up. I often wondered, what the point was with all this inner pain. I couldn't imagine finding normal or close to it. I loved the freedom and the peace, but I still felt like I wasn't a part of life, only playing a part. The ebb and flow of the Pacific Ocean lulled me. I spent hours by the water. I had a large rock where I would sit and write. I would wade to my rock when the tide was out with my paper and pencils in my hand, until it came back in. I'd been writing poetry for years before coffee houses began to flourish, and in the 1960's, poetry readings gave me a space to share my thoughts. Most of my poetry was raw and depressing, in many ways therapy before therapy was in vogue. Eventually, I sauntered off the beach and landed at the Bunkhouse, a coffee house on Davie Street. I was the very image of a 1960s flower-child poet, long blonde hair, black clothing and a beret. It was an experimental decade, smoking anything and everything was in. I added a pipe to my persona with aromatic tobacco I bought on Granville Street. I never did light it or smoke, it was just a prop. We were poets, singers, and musicians, from all corners of the globe.

A few of the first performers I hung out with in the Green Room were already established artists.

Two of my favourites were, Sonny Terry and Brownie McGhee. Sonny Terry had performed in New York at Carnegie Hall, and broke into folk music with Brownie McGee, along with musicians such as Josh White and Woody Guthrie. In 1965 they recorded a blues album at the Bunkhouse. I was the youngest regular freelance poet at the Bunkhouse, and they were always encouraging and friendly, giving me a spot. One night I ran into a blind singer, Jose Feliciano in the Green Room who was at the beginning of his career. A favourite was a talented, young draft dodger from Kentucky. His fingers flew over his banjo like wildfire when he played, "The Flight of the Bumblebee." He had crossed the border to avoid the draft during the Vietnam War. He told me his father was a member of the Ku Klux Klan, and he wanted no part of it. We became friends, and we spent many hours talking about life until he expressed an interest in me romantically. I wasn't interested in a relationship with anyone at that time, dating wasn't on my radar. About that time, a young Ann Mortifee made a musical debut at the Bunkhouse too. I remember seeing her standing waiting with her guitar. Later, she would later perform at Carnegie Hall, and record at Abbey Road. Years later, she wrote the musical score for Margaret Atwood's film, 'Surfacing.' She also worked with Mother Teresa in India and was awarded the Order of Canada and the Queen's Jubilee Medal. Her way of relating to the world, as I later watched from afar, was something I could only dream of. Even if the brass ring was in front of me, I was too terrified to grab it. Many years later I knit her a Superwoman sweater after a long night of drinking wine at The Arts Club in Vancouver, after her show, 'Reflections on Crooked Walking.'

While artists, writers, and musicians around me flourished, I continually stopped myself from moving forward. I lacked a foundation. I floated in an uncertain universe. The Bunkhouse was one the first public experiences I had where I felt part of something where I had value. Although I lacked confidence in my ability to fit in, I knew that as a poet, I had some credibility. Nights were spent on the beach with musicians jamming until the sun rose. There were bonfires blazing not far from the dark lapping waters of the Pacific Ocean. My older brother was now a talented guitar player and singer living in Montreal. When he was in Vancouver, I would join him and his circle. The gentle lyrics of folk music always carried me to a perfect place.

One day I made a friend sitting on the grass by English Bay. Ava was alone, holding a clarinet. She told me her parents owned a large house near the beach. We began a conversation and found we were easy with one another. She asked me where I lived, and I told her nowhere steady. It appeared we were both looking for a friend and she took me home. She told her parents that I was moving in, and that was that. They looked at her and said, that's fine with us.

My new friend was serious and introspective. We spent hours singing at the top of our lungs to Joan Baez, in Ava's dining room. Her father showed up on occasion; the owner of an export company, he was often away, and her mother rarely came out of her suite. The housekeeper cooked our meals and cleaned our rooms. Ava had sporadic contact with her parents, other than them shoving money into her hands whenever she asked for it. We hauled nets to the water at night to catch smelt, sometimes sleeping on the beach. We would wade out waist-deep into the ocean in the morning, collecting our catch. We sold the smelt we caught to the residents in one of the apartment buildings her parents owned.

This was a respite for me, I had a warm bed and food. Ava and I became cautious friends. Although we shared our love of music, her room and writing, we weren't close. It appeared that we were both wary of trust. When I look back, her parents were probably relieved I moved in, so they needn't feel guilty about their daughter being alone. That was my first realization that loneliness lives everywhere. Ava had a beautiful black lab, Laddie. I loved that dog, and he became my constant companion when I was feeling alone.

One summer evening while I was walking behind the recently opened, 'Playhouse Theatre Company,' I noticed a long line-up. I walked over, and life took another unexpected turn.

"What's happening here?"

The first young woman I spoke to informed me she'd travelled from San Francisco for the audition. She looked at me standing there empty handed.

"Do you have a monologue prepared?"

I was standing there with nothing in my hands, while the din of actors trying to recall their lines permeated the air.

"I knew that line, I know that line, why can't I remember it?"

There was frustration and nervousness as each would-be actor moved closer to the front. Two directors were shuffling the hopefuls forward. I wasn't nervous because I had no expectations and didn't realize the importance of the audition. I wasn't even on the list; I was just a curious young woman wandering past. After a good half-hour in the line, I came face-to-face with a director. He noted that my hands were empty.

"Do you have something prepared?"

"No, I was just walking by, saw the line-up and…"

Before I could finish, he thrust a page of dialogue in front of me.

"Read this."

I read the page of dialogue with the director, and he pulled out another page.

"Now read this."

I filled out some papers with my information and left. The following week, I learned I was one of those chosen to participate in the acting apprenticeship program at the Playhouse Theatre Company. Our director was a wonderful man I would meet decades later again in Toronto, Malcolm Black. After my role as Jo in, 'A Taste of Honey,' Malcolm encouraged me to apply to The National Theatre School but my life went quickly in a different direction. My time at The Playhouse was my first group experience outside of school with my peers, and I felt like the classic square peg in a round hole. Most of them still lived with their families, and I was staying at the house of a stranger I'd met on the beach. They talked about their friends and their future plans, while I had none.

I was in awe of 'normal' and the lives they talked about. I'd been sur-
viving for the past five years primarily on my own, trying to figure it
out.

One of the first group exercises at the Playhouse involved de-
scribing your best friend. I remember the terror I felt as the others
spoke in the circle. I was wracking my brain for a viable story. It was
an acting workshop, but I was scrambling trying to come up with
something that made sense that wouldn't humiliate me. When my turn
came, I stammered that my best friend was Laddie, a black lab. I lis-
tened while they described relationships I'd never experienced. The
twins had one another. Their story was like a fairy tale to me. Parents
who cared about them and nurtured their talents. They both performed
in school musicals and had everything I'd always dreamed about. One
of them became the principal dancer at the Stuttgart Ballet, and later
the artistic director. They all had something I was missing, an authen-
tic connection and a way of relating to the world that was foreign to
me. I excelled at theatre. Why wouldn't I? I'd been acting all my life.
My first challenge as Jo in, "A Taste of Honey," undressing, and
standing on stage in my underwear, didn't bother me as much as de-
scribing my best friend as a black lab. I met my first true friend at the
Playhouse. Eric Wilson was the epitome of kindness, an awkward red-
head with slightly protruding teeth. He was a few years older than me,
and we were a perfect friend match. I wasn't interested in men in a
romantic sense, although I didn't figure out why until much later. We
talked about going to Scotland the following year, with another actor
named Leslie. She wanted to work at the Edinburgh Festival. I was
still free-falling without a map for my future. I was living one day at a
time, letting life unfold as each new day dawned. The following year
Leslie went to Scotland and never returned. Eric already had a teach-
ing degree and had begun to work. We wrote letters back and forth for
a while, then lost touch. He became a writer and well-known chil-
dren's author for his series, Tom and Liz, Austen. Eventually, he
would sell over a million books in ten languages, and he too would be

a recipient of the Queen's Jubilee Medal. We met up later in life when he was on a book tour. He surprised me when he showed up at a theatre in Nelson BC, where I was playing Eve in, "Waiting for The Parade."

The sixties had a unique vibe that we will never see again. It can be copied but never duplicated. The poets, the musicians, the late-night gatherings on the beach, waves crashing into the rocks playing back up to the songs of the era.

The sixties era was a feeling you could almost taste and touch, we could feel it in the air. On one side, we had Woodstock, Bob Dylan, Joan Baez and other musicians singing protest songs and making us aware through their music. There was a feeling of freedom and celebration, although the Vietnam War hung over us at the same time. The attitude of the young was, if life is going to be short, let's make the most of it. Vancouver was a gathering place for many adventurous young men and women from all around the world. Music, Poetry and love was our salvation. Sitting around crackling fires on the beaches of the Pacific Ocean, we were lulled into a world we created, our love of life palpable. We were, for the most part, optimistic about our unknown futures. Philosophical conversations averted most negativity and our differences. We were a generation who expressed our feelings and weren't afraid to live in the moment. These years would form the core of my being.

One early winter evening, after a rehearsal at the Playhouse, I wandered down to Robson Street, or 'Robson Strasse,' as the locals dubbed it. The area was heavily populated by new residents from postwar Germany, and famous for its numerous German specialty shops. Parts of it felt like an intimate Bavarian village. That night, the snow was falling softly, the streetlamps glowing, and I was feeling alive with the soft flakes landing on my face.

CHAPTER TEN

A New Lonely

Soft snowflakes were covering the sidewalks while Petula Clark's hit song, "Downtown" was filling the airwaves. The evening would be a long one for me. My friend Eric stayed behind at the theatre for his final costume fitting. He wasn't happy about the tunic he was wearing.

"Do you realize I'm wearing a dress?"

He was conservative with his red hair. He was a man I knew I could trust.

"It's not a dress, Eric, it's a tunic."

My costume fitting had been the week before, and I was thrilled with the heavy brown velvet gown and gold braid across the bodice. It was elegant, not a look I usually strived for, preferring my wooden clogs or lace-up gladiator sandals. Onstage for poetry readings I always wore black, a contrast to my blonde hair. My winter attire was a camel duffle coat with wooden toggles.

"That's your definition, we're both wearing dresses."

Eric was like a dog with a bone.

"Hey, enjoy the moment, you know we are going to be onstage with some of the best Shakespearean actors in the country."

We were playing bit parts in, 'Romeo and Juliet,' at The Queen Elizabeth Theatre.

"Did you feel that material, it's scratchy."

I smiled at Eric's innocence. I didn't think there was enough adversity in his life if a scratchy costume was his biggest concern.

I left the theatre and walked over to Georgia Street, where I could purchase a vile of my favourite oil. The Persian store was filled with the aromas from a land I'd only read about. I crossed the street to Christ Church Cathedral, standing solid like a beacon of hope for those who wanted to sit and pray. I stopped for a few minutes to rest and take in the tranquillity. I loved to sit and observe people going about their daily lives. I watched the throngs of people walk by on their way to homes they probably shared with their families. Eventually, I made my way through the snow down Robson Street to say hello to a shop owner I'd met a few months before when I needed a key cut. We'd struck up an unlikely friendship when I had commented on the baby photo on his counter.

"Cute baby, is he yours?"

He picked up the photograph and looked lovingly at his young son.

"Yes, he's almost a year old."

Stuart appeared lonely and sad in his little shop. Often when I came this way I would stop for a chat. We'd sit on the high stools, overlooking the busy street, sip on tea or hot chocolate. Stuart would talk about his life, a life he was resigned to, married to a much older woman who was suspicious of his every move.

"I love the little guy, and I just wish she wasn't so critical, all I ever wanted was a family."

Stuart's wife stopped by one day while I was visiting. I could feel her instant dislike of me. She probably wondered what innocence there could be in a nineteen-year-old sipping tea with her husband in his late thirties. For me, differences in gender just weren't important. Dating and the opposite sex were not on my radar. I was immersed in poetry, theatre and survival, a dandelion blowing in the wind, little pieces of me falling, sprouting, and then floating off into another space. With no return ticket or destination, my writing and acting gave me a reason to keep going. Listening to Stuart's story about the perils of marriage, I thought about my mother, a prisoner of circumstance and economics, and knew that I would never want that for me. I couldn't imagine a life where someone else made all the decisions. I watched my mother's dependence on my father grow, until she faded into shadows of doubt. Above all, I valued my freedom, and was happy with the person I was becoming.

The decision to stop and visit Stuart that blustery December day steered my life in an unexpected direction. We were about to sit down with our mugs of hot chocolate when an acquaintance of his dropped by. Edward was a conservative businessman in an expensive suit. From all outward appearances, he was something I didn't believe in, the establishment. Stuart introduced us, went to the back, and poured another mug.

"Pass this over to Edward, will you?"

The hot cup slipped out of my hands and splashed all over Edward's brown tweed suit, soaking the legs of his pants. He jumped up and pulled the material away from his skin.

"Don't worry, I'm fine."

Stuart was frantic, but Edward was calm.

"Jeez, run and grab a cloth and some water."

"Let's just be careful so no one slips on this."

Edward wiped his pants off as best he could, and later offered me a ride home. I thanked him and declined. I couldn't imagine what we'd have to say to one another. As soon as he left, Stuart felt compelled to relive the scene.

"You're lucky he's a good sport, that could have been a disaster."

I couldn't think of any other way to apologise and simply stated the obvious.

"It was an accident, the mug was hot, and it slipped out of my hands."

Just as I was getting ready to leave, I looked at Stuart and blurted out something that caught both of us by surprise, considering I'd never thought about marriage.

"I'm going to marry him."

Stuart's mouth fell open, and instantly I felt like a fool.

"Good God, you just dumped hot chocolate over him, and have known him for an hour, what are you thinking?"

I heard my own words come back at me, and I was as shocked as Stuart. Where had they come from? Disbelief added to the humiliation.

"He's too old for you, and you wouldn't be his type, he just broke up after a relationship with an accountant."

I pulled my hat on and left, feeling unsettled. I sensed a shift, a premonition, that my life was about to change. Although I'd never even dated, and marriage was the last thing on my radar, I knew this was my destiny for the next chapter.

Christmas was approaching, and I stopped by Robson Street a couple of weeks later to drop off a small gift for Stuart's baby. As luck would have it, Edward also stopped by on the way home from his office, hoping to share a Christmas drink with his friend. I could barely look at him. I was sure that somehow my impulsive words had reached him, although I'd made Stuart promise not to say anything. I was rushing out the door when Edward stopped me and asked if I'd like a lift home. It turned out we lived close to one another. It was another blustery winter evening. This time, I accepted his offer. The conversation on the twenty-minute ride home was sparse. By this time, I was imagining he could read my mind, and when he dropped me off, he caught me off guard.

"Would you like to go out with me on New Year's Eve?"

With my naivety around dating rituals because I'd never dated anyone, I stammered back. "I don't make plans that far in advance, I'm going to spend the holidays with my mom out of town."

His life obviously had a flow, a formality mine lacked. His corporate world would have been scheduled and consistent, I was in free fall. But he persisted.

"My mother lives up north, in the country on a ranch, they have box numbers."

The conversation was awkward and vague. I thanked him for the ride and hopped out, a confused feeling in my gut. The last thing my mother had said to me those years ago when I left was, be sure to write. We kept in constant touch through our letters, hers focused on the ranch. There was a shortage of hay that they could buy to feed the horses and cattle. My younger sibling fell off her pony last week and had to go to the hospital for stitches. Then the ever-present dark cloud. "Your dad is as miserable as ever; Christmas is coming and he doesn't think the kids need toys."

His need to control my mom put unnecessary stress on her. He usually gave her what she needed for the children at Christmas, but not without holding back until the last minute. I made sure that I kept enough from my meager forty dollar a moth living allowance to buy all my siblings Christmas presents to alleviate her stress. She knew she could count on me.

"They have seven hundred acres to play on, why do they need toys?"

My mother was isolated by economics and geography, and powerless to do anything about it, so she made do with what she had, and prepared for the holidays with as much verve as she could muster. She decorated the house, baked pies, tarts, Christmas cakes and puddings. She was happy when I came home to visit and hid her sadness when I left. I did the same, always wishing it could be different for all of us. Being away from his crazy, unpredictable behaviour made me more aware of how dysfunctional my life had been. My mother and I both knew our pain, but it would be decades before we could talk about it openly. I regaled her with interesting stories about my life, leaving out the loneliness I often felt. My father now ignored me since I'd left home. I think he was glad to get rid of me, because I wasn't afraid to stand up to him. Standing up for myself at a young age, meant I paid for it with beatings from belts buckles, steel toed boots and bull whips, but my will to survive appeared to be born into me. He'd come to the conclusion that my tenacity was innate. There was no way he could bully me. This Christmas, my younger siblings welcomed me as usual, scrambling for the gifts I always brought them.

There were lots of hugs, and the little ones vied for my attention. I would have felt like a sister in 'Five Little Peppers and How They Grew,' if my father had been out of the picture. The emotional scars he left on all of us would last for decades. Did I read their latest report cards?

Did I know that their sister had fallen off her pony, and as soon as she got home from the hospital jumped right back on? When was I coming back? Could I read them a story or make one up?

"Come out to the barn and see the new calves!"

Once everyone settled down, I blurted out these words to my mother.

"If I get flowers over the holidays, I'm getting married in the summer."

Once again, where was that voice coming from?

My mom was staring at me with a quizzical look on her face.

"I didn't know you were seeing someone."

"I'm not, I've only met him twice through a friend, but I have a feeling, he asked me out for New Year's and wanted to know where I was going for the holidays."

"That doesn't sound like a marriage proposal to me."

She lit a cigarette and stared at me, the daughter who was a mystery to her. Flowers arrived the following week, a dozen red roses, in dramatic contrast to the relentless winter snow. Finding me in northern British Columbia would not have been easy.

The next visit to my family included Edward. We were engaged to be married in August, and my mother was beside herself. Although she knew I was independent and capable of surviving on my own, she secretly thought that I needed a man to take care of me. Hers was a life of service. Marrying a daughter off was proof of normality for her. My love of poetry, theatre, and hanging out in coffeehouses wasn't a lifestyle she could relate to.

Engagement to be married, she considered, was the first real step towards her oldest daughter's adulthood. Little did she know that I had never been interested in men or dating. In the back of my mind, I felt there was a force bigger than I could control, destiny somehow was driving this, a path that had chosen me rather than me choosing it.

Edward's introduction to the ranch was an eye-opener. He'd grown up in the city of Vancouver and considered Stanley Park the country. His own early life was filled with sadness. His father and uncle had started, and owned, 'The Burnaby Advertiser,' one of the largest newspapers in the B.C. Lower Mainland. At the age of four, as he was walking to his father's office with his mother, she dropped dead of a heart attack and fell on top of him. His father, grief-stricken, died when Edward was in his teens. Father and son had moved in with his aunt and uncle when his mother passed away, and they became his second parents. His uncle won many awards for journalism, and later in life was a very popular mayor of Burnaby for eighteen years. The family had their own box at the races, the key to the city, and a personal invitation to attend a reception and dinner with Queen Elizabeth and Prince Philip. A gentleman bred for formality and convention, Edward was about to be married to a Bohemian, who relished wandering on the beach and sitting in dark coffeehouses with an unlit pipe.

From their first meeting, my mother loved everything about Edward, although she was incredulous that anyone so conservative would be interested in me. I was dreading the moment of introduction, but my mother looked at me as if I'd won the lottery.

"Do you like Pheasant? she inquired."

I'm positive Edward had no idea what was coming, but I knew I needed to let this play out. He answered that he would be happy to eat anything she cared to prepare. I could see that they liked one another instantly, and they would develop a deep affection for one another.

I had scored on that point with her, Edward was a kind, sensitive man. He loved my mother, everyone loved her, except my father.

"I'll be back in about half an hour and cook you that pheasant."

She grabbed one of her guns from the rack beside the door and disappeared. A far cry from sitting with the Queen. She returned a while later with a huge smile on her face and four dead pheasants. She skinned them in the yard, preparing them in record time for dinner. She was in her element, here was someone who appreciated her.

Later, my grandmother Elizabeth found him to be a welcome addition to the family too. We spent many hours visiting her, and she loved to debate with Edward. They would engage in friendly banter over their political differences, with a large portrait of John F. Kennedy hanging over her dining room table as a witness.

My father's family were all city dwellers. They all scoffed at his move to the country. Their attitudes towards him, as the black sheep of the family, always made me feel separated from our paternal relatives. They were conventional and conservative, except for my grandmother and Uncle Willy, who was not like any of them. I was her oldest grandchild, and she shared things with me about the disappointment she felt with some of my aunts and uncles. Their dismissive attitude towards us was like being punished twice for a life beyond our control.

My impending marriage brought about a new rift because of religion. My mother's family all lived far away, while my fathers were in Vancouver, heavily involved with Catholicism. Many of them avoided my wedding because it wasn't in a Catholic church. There was also Edward's very conservative family to deal with. His aunt looked horrified the first time she met me.

There had been a great deal of coaching and preparation from Edward before the day came.

"She will be sitting in the dining room on her chair. Stand by the door and she will let you know when she wants to meet you."

I felt as though I was being prepared to meet the queen. I'm not sure why I went along with it, but I did and kept my mouth shut, but I could feel her disapproval within seconds. When she finally summoned me, I stood in front of her chair. She didn't ask me to sit down, rather she motioned for me to come closer. Then she lifted the hem of my carefully chosen skirt. This was the era of hot pants, little skirts or dresses with matching pants, hipster jeans and flowing gauze dresses. I'd dressed carefully in a conservative dress.

"There's room to let this down, it's too short."

It went downhill from there until I gave birth to my first child, a replica of her father. I was careful to dress for her approval, because it was easier than having her complain to Edward. Before we were married, she gave me a book, 'Married Love,' it was written in the 1800's. I was already questioning this path that seemed to have chosen me. I don't remember being in love, or even knowing how that felt. All I knew was that this was my next step in life, towards what, I wasn't sure. We liked one another and were compatible, read similar books and decided to marry and have children. It wasn't complicated, just not a traditional love story.

Everything about it was surreal: the planning, the wedding, and the expectation that I was going to be a wife. I watched while his family and friends organised everything. His childhood church, his friends, his honour guard made up of miniature soccer players lining the area where we'd walk after the ceremony. He was the director of a large soccer club, and they were there to honour him, wearing their bright orange shirts, all waving flags. I felt like a bystander.

When I arrived, the flower girls were standing on the church steps with empty baskets. I'd forgotten to get them flowers. Since it was August and not December, the churchyard was fortunately overflowing with blossoms. I was an hour late because we couldn't find the church; I was desperately sewing the veil onto my tiara while we drove. After the ceremony, one of my Playhouse Theatre friends sang a solo, 'You'll Never Walk Alone,' from Carousel, one of my favourite musicals. Little did I know how wrong those words were at the time.

It was all a blur, the honeymoon a disaster. The cottage we went to on a remote island was desolate and dreary. Before my marriage had barely begun, I knew it was a mistake. Any loneliness I'd felt during my years on my own was different, it wasn't filled with a longing for the connection I imagined I would feel. On my honeymoon I wrote a poem:

"My words tucked away

My thoughts silent,

I am stretched

Into a fine line. Together with you I am alone.

Alone with you,

I am alone."

Prophetically, I left the marriage just short of twelve years.

CHAPTER ELEVEN

Fifty-Fifty

You will need your husband's permission to get a tubal ligation. I was aghast. After half a decade as a married woman, I was invisible in the eyes of the law. I protested to no avail. I wasn't aware I would be giving up the right to decisions about my body. There was so much I wasn't aware of as a married woman in the sixties.

"They're my tubes, and it's my body."

I hadn't lost my tenacity.

"Sorry, Ma'am, that's the law, we can't do it without his permission."

Like my mother, I hadn't put any forethought into the implications of marriage. I wandered into marriage just as I'd wandered into a line-up at The Playhouse, and then into Stuart's shop, where I dumped hot chocolate all over my future husband. Like my mother, I was seeking refuge from a storm, not thinking about future consequences. Fate or folly, I wasn't sure, but those words that flew unexpectedly out of my mouth when I met Edward, I'm going to marry him, happened for a reason. It was still a mystery.

After we married, I tried to stay involved in performance and auditioned for a musical at Vancouver Little Theatre. I was surprised when they offered me a lead role because I wasn't a strong singer.

After two rehearsals, I quit. The confidence and spark that had carried me into my marriage was waning. My energy was consumed with the new expectations of me as a wife. I was immediately expected to take over the role of his doting aunt.

"I like my collars starched when you press my shirts."

I thought about my mother sweating over the stove and ironing board.

"Well then, you'll need to take them to the dry cleaners."

Our first child, Mandy, was born thirteen months after the wedding. I was ecstatic to be a mother. I'd been practising all my life for this.

The physician who delivered her was a long-time doctor of Edward's family. The doctor commented on how she looked just like her father, her dark curls already evident.

Two years later, our son Jamie was born. He had my fair hair, but as he grew older, looked like his father too. I found children interesting, and I loved being a mother. I read incessantly to them, especially from one of their favourites, naturally, a poetry book.

'Robert Louis Stevenson's A Child's Garden Of Verses.'

New parenting modes began to emerge in the sixties. While the previous decade was rigid, this one carried New Age norms. In our suburb, it was almost a competition. Sandboxes were being replaced with miniature violins; Suzuki was popular for three-year-olds. My two held their miniature violins and played, "Tuka Tuka Ruff Ruff," and, "Go Tell Aunt Rhody," more often than I cared to count. Mandy attended, 'The New School,' when she was four. It was an experimental free-for-all academy brought up from California. On many occasions, we sat through Sesame Street, played fervently with Mr. Dress Up, and tip-toed through the living room, with The Friendly Giant.

Early on, I introduced my children to live theatre and musicals. We sat on the grass in Stanley Park and watched puppet shows, and they swam in the ocean. One summer I was in a large scale musical production, 'The Arts Club.' was staging. My kids were always with me at rehearsals and one day the director was looking for additional children and asked my daughter to join them. She was four, and became addicted to the stage. They cut their teeth on Godspell, Jesus Christ Superstar, and Hair. I bought my own leather at Tandy's on Commercial Drive, and made them tiny, fringed vests and jackets. As toddlers they could run and climb in their trendy wooden clogs, I purchased on Robson street.

Adults were discovering it was in vogue to admit they had feelings, and open marriage was on the rise. Self-awareness and Gestalt groups were crowded with those searching for a higher meaning. Clients could punch pillows under the watchful eye of a therapist for a small fee, while confronting an imaginary spouse, with a one-way conversation. Self-help books flooded the market. If you were depressed or lonely, you could read, 'The Book of Hope.' Body Language made us cautious about crossing our arms or legs. 'The Hite Report.' refashioned sex, and many women wondered what they were missing. Richard Bach's, 'Jonathan Livingstone Seagull,' was there if you were searching for peace.

In the middle seventies, at dinner one night, Edward surprised me out of the blue. It was nearing the end of June.

"Would you be interested in moving to Toronto in August?"

It wasn't really a question. I found out that Edward had already accepted the offer with no discussion. He'd signed over some of his shares in his Vancouver-based import-export company to his best friend, and business partner. He had been asked to open a branch of a friend's company in Toronto, combining it with the existing

Vancouver business he was part of. In early August I landed with the children at Pearson Airport on a hot humid day.

"How does anyone breathe here?"

That was my first impression of Toronto after living on the West Coast.

"You'll get used to it."

He'd come a month earlier. A split-level house waited for us on a quiet cul-de-sac, in Oakville. Mandy, who had already started treading the boards in Vancouver, was signed immediately with Characters Agency, and within two weeks making her first appearance at CBC on a Sesame Street segment. This was a serious business in Toronto, not as relaxed as it had been in the West. Not wanting a career as a stage mother, I hired a manager to communicate with Mandy's agent, take her to auditions and to work. We were settling into a new normal. In December we got our first taste of a winter blizzard. We spent an adventurous day tramping around a farm, looking for the perfect Christmas tree. The snow was relentless, and by evening it had piled up on our driveway and sidewalks. The tree was downstairs in the family room, waiting to be decorated after dinner when Edward said he wasn't feeling well, and went to lie down. He called me almost immediately.

"Can you come quickly, I'm getting chest pains."

This was news. He'd never complained of chest pain before. He was thirty-six years old and, I thought, healthy. I went up the six stairs to the bedroom and looked at him.

"I'm calling the doctor."

The call was futile. The Doctor wasn't too concerned, and I still sensed there was something wrong. The unconcerned voice on the other end irritated me.

"Give him an Aspirin and bring him in to emergency tomorrow."

I walked back to check on him and his face was ashen. I gathered all the physical strength I had to get him off the bed, down the stairs and out to the car. I left eight-year-old Mandy in charge because I didn't know anyone in my neighbourhood I could call.

"If you need anything, go knock on a neighbour's door."

There was no time for me to explain, or grab a coat, or gloves. The car was covered in thick snow, the front window iced over, the wiper blades frozen in place. I clawed at the windshield with my hands, just enough to allow me to drive. At the hospital, a ten-minute drive away, I again found strength I didn't know I possessed to get him into the emergency room.

"Hurry please, I think my husband's having a heart attack."

No one hurried, and they began to ask me mundane questions.

"For God's sake, please take him in."

I could see how frightened he was. I made enough of a fuss that they took him in, and after a long wait a nurse came out to tell me he was fine. She made a feeble attempt to put my fears at rest.

"We've done some tests, and he's not having a heart attack."

Relieved I waited for him to appear. A few minutes after the conversation with the nurse I'd just spoken to, I heard a huge commotion behind the closed doors. I sat in the waiting room for what seemed to be a long time.

Finally, a young female doctor came into the waiting room and took me to her private office.

"Your husband arrested four times."

I just stared at her mouth, watching her words fall into the empty space that had suddenly become my life. She delivered the news flatly.

"He has significant muscle damage to his heart."

Speechless, I listened.

"His chances of surviving the night are fifty-fifty."

I could barely get out the words, and I felt like I was in a bad dream.

"Is he going to die?"

"The odds are not good, if he makes it through the night, he has a fifty percent chance."

Then she stood up and opened the door. Not, I'm sorry, or do you need to talk to someone.

"I'll call you if anything changes."

That was it. On our first winter solstice in Ontario, I stumbled blindly out to my car, exhausted and in disbelief. What would I tell my children three days before Christmas Eve? There was noone to talk to, and no support here in Ontario for any of us. I put my head down on the steering wheel and heard a loud piercing scream. It was coming from me. The green telephone on the kitchen wall remained silent while I slept on a kitchen chair, waiting for fifty-fifty all through the night. The next few days were a blank. I don't remember the tree, the children or Christmas. Although Edward and I didn't have much in common as a married couple, he was my best friend, and I cared about him deeply. We discussed politics, the books we read, and our children.

About four years into our marriage, we were sitting in Stanley Park watching our two young children roll in the fall leaves, when he surprised me.

"I think you're gay."

In the early seventies, gay wasn't a word spoken out loud often. In retrospect, he named it before I did. Although I always felt more comfortable with women, I had no point of reference for my feelings. I was born into a world where women were taught to serve men.

"What makes you say that?"

When I first met him, I wondered if he might be gay. I was at The Playhouse Theatre company when we met, my first exposure to anyone who might be gay. It was his feminine qualities that first appealed to me, his soft speaking voice, his quiet sensitivity, and the gentle way he cared for his elderly aunt and uncle. I'd always gravitated to girl crushes when I was very young, not knowing what they meant.

Our lives changed significantly after Edward's heart attack, on December 21st, in Toronto. From the beginning, he resisted medical advice, which led to frustration for all of us, and within a month he was working from home. We moved out of our house into a manageable townhome where we didn't have snow removal and lawns to take care of. I rarely left Edward alone during the next six months. I was afraid if I did, I would come home and find him dead. He had one more scare after the initial attack and was taken to the hospital in an ambulance. When he returned home, he continued to defy his doctor's orders, eventually going back to work at his office. His personality began to change with these new medical realities. I could understand his frustration, but not the denial of his condition, and pushing himself to unrealistic limits his doctors warned him about. I offered him a respite for all of us, a move to somewhere where we could raise our children in a less stressful environment.

I was becoming desperate for adult company. Shortly after we'd moved into our new home after his heart attack, a neighbour slipped an invitation into my mailbox. I carelessly tossed it into a junk drawer and forgot about it. After Edward returned to work at his office, I realised I needed to make some friends. I searched desperately for the forgotten invite; it felt like a lifeline to something normal. The next day I met Nicky, my neighbour, a new friend who would be instrumental in moving my life forward in another direction. After a gathering at her home, Nicky called and invited me to drive to Niagara-on-the-Lake to meet her friend. Two days later we drove to a quaint restaurant in Niagara- On- the Lake. In The Olde Angel Inn Nicky introduced me to her best friend, and female lover. Both women had husbands and children, and the two families were best friends. They had all migrated from Britain to work for a large corporation in Ontario. Seeing the two women together made me aware that my husband was probably right.

"I think you could be gay."

Nicky and her female lover had begun their relationship because their husbands wanted to, 'swing,' with another couple. The two women fell in love. It was certainly an unusual arrangement, but it appeared to work for everyone. The husbands were still friends, and the two families spent much of their free time together, with five young children between them. Edward surprised me by readily embracing Nicky as my gay friend, and they developed a deep affection and friendship. Nicky and her lover were so easy with one another, and both were attentive and loving mothers. Coming out of the relaxed attitudes of the sixties, this arrangement wasn't so shocking.

Meanwhile, Edward was going full speed, ignoring the doctor's orders to take it easy. It was a huge point of contention for me; I felt a responsibility to keep him alive. He was the father of my children, and a wonderful human being. Whether we were a couple or not didn't factor into wanting him in my life, I cared about him.

His sensitivity and kindness were apparent when he honoured an early request from a young Jamie, who had inherited his father's sensitivity.

"Dad, a boy in my class just moved here from Argentina, and his dad needs a job, do you think you could hire him?"

Two weeks later, Claudio's dad had a job in the warehouse.

Edward was relaxed about me spending time with Nicky. I wasn't a bar or party person, but it was interesting to go to gay clubs and see women dancing together. I knew I was hovering on the periphery of a lifestyle I wanted someday for myself, but I was torn and didn't see anyway my life could change easily.

I began to sink into a deep depression. I'd grown up and lived with adversity and managed for the most part to rise above it, but this was different. I couldn't walk out the door the way I had when my father burned my books. Edward was on a fast train to self-destruction, and there was nothing I could do to help him. It was as though he knew his time was limited, and he was determined to do it his way, despite the consequences. He disregarded the doctor's orders to attend the cardiac health space, he continued to smoke, drink too much Scotch, and work longer than he needed to. Our children were only six and eight, and I was afraid they would grow up without their father. Edward and I were living side by side in the same house, we had both acknowledged that our marriage wasn't a conventional one, but we hadn't figured out how to move on.

I felt stuck, his heart damage hanging over us like a dark, ominous cloud. I couldn't leave him and I struggled with the knowledge that my personal needs couldn't be a consideration. How could I be so selfish as to want a life of my own? I couldn't see a future for myself, and I fell deeper and deeper into a bottomless pit. I spent weeks in my room when the children were at school, lost in a numb fog.

I could barely function, I had no hope, ate very little and felt as though all life was drained out of me. Music was the only thing that kept me alive. Carole King's 'You've Got a Friend,' played over and over on my record player. The lyrics, 'Call on me, and I'll be there,' kept hitting me in the heart. I had no close friends other than Nicky, and she had gone back to England for a few months. I saw one doctor who prescribed the drug Lithium. Derived from the Greek word for stone, it described me perfectly, and almost killed me. One day at my lowest point, I finally willed myself to pick up the phone to change my life.

Theatre had been one of my lifelines in Vancouver, perhaps it could be here in Toronto too. Our daughter Mandy was a dedicated child actor by this time appearing in dozens of commercials and working at CBC, while our son Jamie was excelling at horseback riding and tennis. It was obvious early on, he was athletic. After his first ski lesson when he was six, he stayed behind and was coming down the hill on his own when we picked him up. His exceptional English riding skills landed him a small part in the film, 'Equus,' with Richard Burton.

Gradually, I began to make small strides. I took some classes with Eli Rill, the American director and actor who had opened a studio in Toronto. I signed up for Improv at Second City, in order to meet other adults with similar interests. An elite women's club in Toronto, '21 McGill,' became a place of refuge, a space where I could forget about the outer world, for a few hours at least. The large pool, where bathing suits were optional, was the perfect ending to a day. It wasn't unusual to encounter Margaret Atwood, or Sylvia Tyson lounging in the club. We club members rarely discussed our husbands or children, and the connections I made at 21 McGill were not authentic. Many of us appeared to be playing the same role. At the club, many of the wives pretended to have near-perfect lives at home. Once we entered the doors of the club, life appeared perfect, and it was the ideal place to forget our real lives.

The posh restaurant with perfect male waiters, the boutique where we could purchase overpriced clothing. It wasn't the place to show weakness or vulnerability, it was my own little bubble of denial.

Our family, while still intact, was going in different directions. That summer, Mandy was the only child singer on, 'Catch a Rising Star,' with Tommy Hunter, and Dinah Christie. She made commercials with Lorne Greene and Andrea Martin. Later she auditioned with Michael Douglas for a film, and at the same time was offered the role of, 'Baby June,' in, 'Gypsy,' at the Neptune Theatre, in Halifax, the stage her first choice. Her manager flew to Halifax with Mandy to begin rehearsals, while Edward and I decided to take Jamie a week later. We would spend our first holiday together with the kids. While she was at rehearsals, we explored the East Coast, anywhere within a day's driving distance of the city. We went to Peggy's Cove and bought Jamie a replica of, 'The Blue Nose,' miniature lobster traps, and maps of Oak Island. It was the closest we ever came to a family holiday. It was to be our first, and last holiday as a family.

Rita Howell, an actress from Stratford, played Mama Rose in Gypsy. One day a cast member called me over, cautioning me in a whisper.

"Stay away from Rita, she's a lesbian."

Later, Rita and I became friends, and wrote letters back and forth, hers with hand-painted postcards. Meeting, and getting to know Rita as a friend, convinced me I was gay.

Back in Toronto, I was out of my deep depression. One day after Nicky and I were at 21 McGill for lunch, and a bottle of fine wine, we were walking by a house and heard women laughing. We decided to check it out, and unknowingly walked into the meeting of a lesbian ball team, "The Amazons." They said later, that they all thought we were a couple of housewives who were lost.

The last Christmas we spent together as a normal family, was a disaster. We had plans to put up our Christmas tree when their dad came home from work, and the children were waiting eagerly for him to get home. Eight o'clock came, and there was no sign of him. I tried to cut the bottom of the tree off, so the kids and I could fit it into the stand. I was sawing it with a bread knife when I broke down in tears. The children were in their pyjamas, ready for bed.

"Get your coats on, we're going for a drive."

I ushered them into the car, driving to the restaurant I knew Edward went to with his staff. I walked in, kids in tow. There was my husband, laughing and drinking with his staff and secretary, oblivious to the rest of the world. I knew at that moment that I was done. I was following in my mother's footsteps. What I needed wasn't important to anyone, I needed to find my own life again.

Soon after, I told my husband I wanted to move out. I was always upfront with him and we both already knew that separating was inevitable. It never seemed to be the right time, but would there ever be a right time? I was in my early thirties now, and I knew I'd had enough. As the doctors had predicted, Edward had become increasingly irritable after his heart attack, not the relaxed mellow man I once knew. I could understand his frustration and depression; his family history of heart disease couldn't be ignored, and the odds were not in his favour. I had compassion for him, but at the same time, I wanted a life where I could find happiness. He was not inclined to help himself, and I couldn't be responsible for his choices any longer.

It would be the following summer when I moved out, and all of our lives were about to change. That summer Mandy was invited to ride in a parade alongside female impersonator, Craig Russell.

She wore a miniature feather boa matching Craigs. Mandy's final time at CBC would be on, 'Morningside,' with Peter Gzowski, reading from, 'Anne of Green Gables,' with Don Herron. She'd recently been called back to New York by Scott Rudden, her second audition for the musical, 'Annie,' on Broadway. Her short illustrious career was coming to an end.

The day before Edward passed away, he'd put our daughter on a plane to meet me in St Petersburg, Florida. She'd just finished a long run playing Helen Keller, in, 'The Miracle Worker,' at Young Peoples Theatre, with New York director Marty Fried. Author, William Gibson attended one of the performances in Toronto, with two plays being staged.

Florida was hot and humid. I was getting ready to go to bed when I heard a police radio outside the window. I instinctively knew it was for me. I was standing at my open door as the officers came down the hall. The officer solemnly delivered his message.

"We have some bad news for you, your husband is in the hospital, and it doesn't look like he's going to make it."

I left immediately, concerned about Jamie, who was alone at home with his dad. I called a relative who worked for my husband. He was at the hospital with him, and I asked him about my son. He told me Jamie was sitting in the waiting room alone. I asked him to take him in to see his dad, and he refused. Then I said, tell Edward I love him. The shock that he was going to die was overwhelming.

"I can't do that either."

The funeral was a blur, we were all in shock. My children lost their father, and I lost a friend. Although we were not suited to be a married couple, my husband was a kind, sensitive man, who loved and was proud of his children. Apart from our differences, we had a mutual respect. As I flew across the country, I found out on one of my layovers that he'd already passed away. Nine-year-old Jamie was watching, 'Mutiny on The Bounty,' with his dad when he began to have trouble breathing; our son called for a neighbour who took him to the hospital. He never saw his father alive again.

Knowing that someone has a terminal illness, or a condition that will eventually lead to death is one thing, but there is no preparation for when it happens. Walking through the funeral home, picking out a casket planning to bury the father of my children, was like a bad nightmare. Mandy and Jamie decided on the music to be played at the service. Terry Jack's hit, Seasons in the Sun, and, The Carpenters, On Top of The World, echoed back to the days they sang in the living room with their dad.

The first time I walked into the viewing room with my kids was surreal. Jamie walked right over to the coffin looking down at his dad who appeared to be sleeping. With his usual dry wit, he looked at me and said, "What if he sat up and said April fools? It was, in fact, April 1st. A few of Edward's friends came from Vancouver along with his only brother, wanting to know if he'd left him anything in his will. His brother didn't know our children. He had never shown an interest in being part of our lives. I made numerous attempts before we left British Columbia to have a relationship with them, and then we lost touch completely. Right after the service I was approached by an employee from the funeral home.

"What would you like to do with his ashes?"

I looked at him dumbfounded. There was no preparation for this, no point of reference. Our twelve-year marriage could be seen as fleeting in terms of time, but death was eternal. Edward and I began our lives together as a young couple who had one thing in common, we both wanted children, and there were family expectations for both of us, that we find a partner. It wasn't a traditional love story. He was still a very conservative businessman, and I was a poet who only had freedom on her mind. His very conservative elderly aunt and uncle were pressuring him to get married. I came along at the right time. I was not what they expected or even wished for, however after our children were born, they fell in love with being grandparents to them. We both loved our children, however they spent most of their time alone with me. He was a workaholic and didn't get to spend as much time as he might have, but we made some wonderful memories when we could. Jamie was on the soccer field as soon as his dad could find shoes that fit him. When Mandy was born, I teased Edward that her first word would be goalpost because we spent so much time on a soccer field. Flashes of our lives together were going through my mind. His sudden death was still a shock and surreal. We were all just moving in what felt like slow motion. I answered as honestly as I could.

"I don't know, I've never buried anyone before."

My mind was on Jamie, who slid his Blue Jay's cap under his father's lifeless hand, and Mandy, who slipped in a photograph of the three of them at the Toronto Zoo, taken when we'd arrived in Toronto. I wasn't being callous. At the age of 32, this was the first funeral where I'd been in charge. Dealing with my young children, picking out a casket, the shock, I didn't need more questions. I also harboured some regrets. Regret for not being the wife he wanted, and perhaps regret for getting married in the first place, trying to fit into a life where I didn't belong. Regret and anger, that he didn't care enough to listen to the urgent advice of his cardiologist. Regret that he wouldn't be here for his children. Later, I learned that Edward had his first minor heart attack when he was only nineteen. His mother dead at thirty-two, his father in his forties. There was an ominous genetic pattern here, and after his major cardiac arrest, he'd survived for three years on borrowed time. Because we weren't living together, everyone treated me like a pariah which added to my stress. The circumstances around his fatal heart attack would have lasting emotional implications for his children.

I was in shock but somewhat prepared. The year after his heart attack I decided to consult a psychic. During my life I've had numerous

incidents where I was surprised by my own intuition and acute aware-
ness around events. I'd heard great things about a psychic, Geraldine
Smith. I made an appointment with her for a reading, my reality
caught between my strong beliefs in science and the other world.
From an early age I knew that my brain was powerful in terms of my
survival and that there must be a connection to another consciousness
not yet discovered.

I knew I was going to marry my husband as soon as I met him. I knew
he was going to send me flowers and we'd marry in the summer. So
many of these events happened to me and now I wanted some hard
truths. Geraldine and I hit it off right away, there were unspoken ac-
knowledgements that in some ways, we were birds of a feather. I
wasn't concerned about disclosing information that could give me an
inaccurate reading. I was struggling with the fact that I was gay and
wanted out of the marriage and a husband who was hell bent on self
destruction. Right now, she was all I had. She shared that she normally
didn't disclose an imminent death to her clients but told me that my
husband would pass away before three years if he didn't listen to his
doctors. Then she astounded me when she said I would move to
British Columbia and purchase a pyramid type structure. He passed
away about two years into his illness. I purchased a partially con-
structed house on twelve acres in British Columbia. It was owned by
two gay men, a concert pianist and a Botanist. It was multi levelled
and stood high on a hill of bedrock, my new foundation. I had a deck
built over the driveway so no one could drive up to my house. There
was a clearing about thirty feet down the step incline for anyone to
park.

Megan standing at English Bay in Vancouver BC

*Megan at English Bay in
Vancouver BC beside her
writing rock.*

Brother and Megan at Jericho Beach
Vancouver BC in the 60s

Megan in Vancouver BC.　　*Megan on her way to the*
Bunkhouse in Vancouver
BC to read poetry

Megan at PlayHouse Theater Company Vancouver - Romeo and Juliet.

JUN · 65 ·

Megan with Laddie

CHAPTER TWELVE

Letting Go

My late husband's business partners were determined to see me penniless raising two children. After a legal battle I couldn't afford, I received enough money to buy a house, a car, and take care of my children for a few years. There wasn't much left over for extras, but we managed. Not long after his dad passed away Jamie taped a sign to his bedroom door. In bold letters, it sent a clear message.

"LONE WOLF KEEP OUT."

I purchased a home in British Columbia, just as Geraldine Smith had predicted. We were all looking for a new normal, away from the noise and confusion of the large city.

Jamie came home from school one day, with a smile on his face, excited.

"I made a new friend today, Jimmy Salinas, he's from the Philippines and doesn't have any friends here either."

So began a new friendship between two ten-year-old boys, both removed from their former lives. Jamie always managed to find a place to build a fort, and we had a large tree beside our house that was perfect for the two of them. Soon there was a crude tree fort, made from left over plywood. It was their private spot to reflect on life. During the winter the boys went skating on a nearby pond and made snow forts in our backyard. I was so relieved that he'd made a new friend so quickly. Life is unpredictable, as adults know, but loss for children isn't easy.

One day after school I spotted Jamie coming up the driveway very slowly, his arm periodically brushing over his eyes. As he came closer, I could see his tears. He walked into the kitchen and could barely get the words out.

"Jimmy Salinas is moving back to the Philippines, and I'll never see him again, just like dad."

The pain a mother feels for her children when they are hurt is unfathomable. As adults, we quickly learn that nothing is certain, but for children, loss can be a dark hole, with no end in sight. As adults, we know that life eventually leads to death, and sorrow can lead to discovery. That can take years to accept. This was our first Christmas without their dad, and the kids were rummaging through our old box of decorations. Jamie pulled something familiar out of the box.

"Look, here's Dad's Christmas stocking."

He turned it over and ran his finger over his five-year-old printing.

"To dad, from your son."

"Mom, can I give Dad's stocking to Jimmy Salinas so he won't forget me?"

His sister Mandy stared at him.

"You can't give Dad's stocking away just because he died."

"Dad probably wouldn't want to leave it sitting in a box," Jamie replied.

He reluctantly put it back and went to his room. He returned a short time later with a small box.

It was wrapped in leftover paper from last year. "How does it look I took the ripped edges off."

He held it out and turned it over.

"Mom, do we have any scotch tape?"

I opened my junk drawer, remnants of mine, and everyone else's things that probably should have been thrown out, expired coupons, picture hangers, my tomato shaped pin cushion from grade eight home economics, the pins in it probably original. When I removed the red thread that was wound around it, I set the scotch tape free and handed it to Jamie, waiting patiently.

"What's in the box, his sister wanted to know."

Jamie was biting down hard on his bottom lip.

"It's the eagle necklace grandma gave me after dad died, I want to give it to Jimmy, so he doesn't forget me."

The gift of remembrance represented a new strength to Jamie, it was a fine line between holding on, and letting go. While it is human nature to want to hold onto things and people we love, we need the strength to be able to let them go.

Searching throughout the small B.C. communities, nothing felt right. I'd decided to move back to a small town in the county where we could have space and begin a new chapter. Exhausted and almost ready to give up, I drove through the Kootenays, where big horn sheep dotted the rolling hills, and eagles and osprey were abundant. In Grand Forks, I stopped for lunch, ready to make my way back home. None of the small communities where I searched for a new home felt right, and I had given up, on my way back to the North. There was a realtor beside the café, and I decided to go in and take one last look.

As soon as he showed me the listings, I spotted my house. In that moment, I knew I had found my new home.

The psychic had painted a picture of the house I would live in after his death. And now, in the realtor's office, I was looking at it. The realtor tried to talk me out of it.

"I don't think you'd be interested in this property, it's not finished, no one has lived in it for several years, there's a long quarter-mile steep rutted driveway, I don't think you'd even get your car up there."

Nothing he said mattered, I knew this was my property, and I insisted on seeing it.

"I'll show it to you then."

We drove out in my car, we parked at the bottom of the property, and I made my way up the steep long driveway with the realtor, trudging through muddy ruts. I was in awe of the majestic Tamarack trees all around me. At the top, I saw my house, my new home.

"I'll take it."

He looked at me incredulously.

"Don't you want to see inside?"

It didn't matter what it looked like. Standing on the rocks, overlooking a beautiful valley and a rolling river, whatever was inside wasn't important.

"Sure, but this is my house."

He reiterated that there was no running water. I wasn't concerned. I reminded him. "We passed a creek below, and there is a river close by, there's water somewhere, I'll find it."

We drove back to town, and I wrote him a cheque for the entire amount, maybe the easiest sale of his career. One of the former owners had careened over a huge cliff on a narrow spot on the road from town. There were large drops down to the winding Granby River and no guard rails. Although I had become accustomed to driving through perilous canyons in British Columbia, I would always hold my breath at that spot.

I didn't know it at the time, but we had landed in a large Doukhobor community. All I knew about this much-maligned group were comments my mother had made in the fifties, along with others with no knowledge about their history.

"What's wrong with those crazy people, taking off their clothes and setting fires to things?"

Media accounts perpetuated that attitude for decades, with no historical explanation. Once we settled in, I learned that these people were pacifists who were persecuted in Czarist Russia until they were allowed to leave the country. As an admirer of the great Russian writer Leo Tolstoy, I was delighted to learn that Tolstoy helped finance the Doukhobors' migration to Canada. He contributed all the royalties from one of his books, not Anna Karenina, or War and Peace, but a more obscure novel titled, aptly, Resurrection. My oldest granddaughter is half Doukhobor, so now I have a personal connection to the community. A highlight of her young life, and mine, was meeting Leo Tolstoy's great-great-grandson, Vladimir Tolstoy, at the Hundred-year anniversary of the group's migration to Canada.

Her photo with him and the essay she wrote was on the front page of the local paper.

The community's early years in Canada were very difficult.

The Canadian government offered them harsh lands, which they eventually turned into lush orchards. They were promised that they wouldn't be called to do military duty, a promise rescinded when war broke out. The B.C. government demanded they send their children to English schools when they had hoped to home-school them in Russian. Singing their Psalms was a cornerstone of their culture. A sect of the Doukhobors, the Sons of Freedom, refused to comply, and the government began to forcibly remove their children, the R.C.M.P. arriving unannounced at all times of the day and night. The frightened children were placed in camps not far from where the Japanese Canadians had been interned in New Denver, B.C.

A friend of mine gave me a letter written by her husband's mother. Her husband was hunted down at the age of six by the RCMP.

This was a barbaric and cruel practice, for these families who only wanted to be left alone to raise their children as they saw fit. The child's mother saw them coming early that morning. These are her words:

"I see a big bunch of police, most with rubber clubs. They asked me, where is your small boy? I knew he was playing someplace around the house. I just hoped and prayed to God he would be safe... one came up to me and said, your boy is under the house, call him out, or we will break your house. Then I heard the breaking noises, it was like they were breaking the foundation. Then after a while I heard a scream, Mamma, Mamma, Papa, for help. They chased him from corner to corner, with sticks and hoes. One of the police said God gave us permission to gather all the Kootenay Sons of Freedom children to New Denver. Then the police carried my small child to the police car. When I saw my little boy, he looked frightened, with shining eyes, and with a stuttering voice was saying, Goodbye Mamma, Goodbye Papa. He had blood on his forehead, and his chin. And he was saying, please police, let my Mamma ride with me...

It was over a week before my first visit at the camp in New Denver to see my little boy over the fence."

The frustration the Sons of Freedom felt at this treatment led to them taking off their clothing, to show that they had no regard for anything outside the spiritual self. They burned their own houses, and, later, some government offices in protest. Grand Forks is a quaint little town with two gentle rivers flowing through it, and amongst the tranquillity, many stories are hidden in its history, some of them invidious.

We moved into our new home, which I named Pentimento, after one of my favourite authors, Lillian Hellman. Soon our property was overrun with rabbits, the offspring of the two bunnies I'd given my children as their first Easter present in their new home. There was ample space for everything, and the rabbits soon blended in with the numerous deer, hiding from the wolves and the bears. My children made friends with kids their ages, with unusual melodic names, such as Liddy Solstice Prairie Woman, Shimmer, Maisy, Ona, and Meadow. Numerous free-spirited people moved to Canada from the United States after the Vietnam War and settled in this valley. Shimmer's father, Doug, became one of my good friends. He was the first to wander up my driveway shortly after we moved in to introduce himself. His youngest son, Trenin, about three, eyed me carefully. He had an angelic face, and his bright blue eyes were intense. Trenin looked up at me and asked me boldly.

"Do you eat meat?"

A variety of artists and writers lived in the hills, away from the din of city life. One house I visited was built into the earth. There was a stream winding through the living room. It appeared to be the perfect place for my children to heal.

The first winter was a lesson in survival. We had no running water or well. We hauled our water up the steep hill from the spring below on sleds. I'd hired someone to do renovations before we moved in, but when we arrived at spring break, excited to move in, we discovered he'd been spending our money on parties and alcohol. We finished the inside ourselves with tongue-and-groove cedar, built a staircase to our loft, and in the fall, put on a new roof. At the end of each day, there was a feeling of contentment and accomplishment. Our neighbour, Andy, a lifelong resident of the area for more than seventy years, gave us a rod to heat our bathwater, and along with his wife Betty, befriended us immediately. Andy taught me to measure three times and cut once and loaned us his tools. Mandy found a new friend with their late in life daughter, Sandy. The following spring Andy doused our property, we found water, and dug a deep well. Our house was built on bedrock, and that was its only foundation. There was a kitchen, a small bathroom with an organic compositing toilet, and three bedrooms on the ground floor level. We turned what had been the dining room into a library. The loft, all windows, looked out across the valley, and a river. A Canadian National Railway train wound through the mountain, across the valley. It was picturesque, and tranquil, with a million-dollar view. Jamie was in his physical element. For a lover of animals and nature, there was ample room to build bike ramps, ski down the driveway, and eventually, create a pet cemetery. The winter was full upon us, and our reward was memories for a lifetime. Walking down the hill in the evenings through our property, large fluffy snowflakes landed like soft feathers on our faces. Through the trees with moonlit skies and stars above, we trekked, a brush with an occasional tree branch depositing cold snow down our necks. We made new friends and drank hot chocolate together in front of a roaring fire in a cabin in the woods. We marvelled at the simplicity of our new existence. Jamie soon made another new friend. Todd and Jamie looked like a Rockwell Painting. They spent their time fishing, poles over their shoulders, carrying a bag of Oreo cookies with Todd's large dog, Jake, lopping along beside them. They swam in the river, and explored the surrounding hills.

Spring brought more treasures. New life around us, a family of squirrels moved into the eaves, and we all gave one another space. Deer slept under our trees with new fawns, and they barely budged when we opened our door. I was in awe of our trees and the transformation of our Tamaracks. Deciduous conifers, they were bright yellow in the fall, their soft blue-green needles lost before the bright yellow bursts. I would stand on the deck and think to myself, these are my trees.

I'd found a nirvana for my children. They embraced their new environment. Being gay at that time in a new community wasn't easy. I tried to fit in, and at times educate those who wondered if we were different from them. One of my son's school friends stands out. He was a very talented athlete and musician, and highly competitive. Mitch came up to my house one day to buy a banjo I was selling. He was very confident, and a bit cocky too. I don't remember our exact conversation, but I remember talking to him about something he said to me. Many years later, I read an email from him. He said, "I remember a conversation we had in your kitchen in Grand Forks when I was a troubled teenager. I took that as my first self-imposed lesson to be more respectful of diversity. Now I try to create diverse teams. I find that people from diverse backgrounds, united by a common goal, produce better ideas (and better results)"

At the time he wrote that Mitch Higashi was the Chief Economist of GE Healthcare, in Chicago. Now he's the Vice President at Bristol-Myers Squibb.

You were listening, Mitch. We can all find teachable moments. I don't think he was ever troubled, he was just waiting to break free from a small town, so he could become the success he is today. It's another testament to how powerful our words can be.

A few years later, I would meet my partner in this small community. As in any community, we were accepted by some but not everyone. Autumn's parents disowned her, and they remained estranged. Autumn gave her parents a book written by parents of gay offspring, 'Now That You know.' In the margins, her parents wrote, "We would rather she was dead," "God's law, not man's law." There was never going to be a resolution, and my family became hers. My mom loved Autumn and treated her like one of her own. Homophobia was still everywhere. We had a simple life, working, driving the now teenaged kids to drama practices, ski hills, and the occasional road trip. One in particular was memorable, to find Jamie overpriced BMX van shoes, that were all the rage. We drove miles looking for those shoes. Mandy was happy at home with her stacks of library books.

Our early life together was filled with adventures. After the kids left home, we rode our Honda Gold Wing all over the province. One sunny fall day, we decided to ride to the Grand Coulee Dam. It was warm when we left, but we had to stop and borrow warm clothes from friends, Pat and Pauline on our way back because we were freezing. Later we ran out of gas and turned our engine off. We cruised down the long winding summit to Osoyoos in the dark and silence. It was magical looking down at the lights of the town shimmering across the lake with the stars overhead.

Eventually, we moved to Toronto to be close to Autumn's aunt and uncle. They accepted her immediately when she came out as a lesbian, and Autumn said her aunt was more like a mother to her. Autumn was her aunt's goddaughter.

Autumn took a course in theatre lighting and landed some interesting positions at The Metro Convention Centre in Toronto. One of them was the Canadian Country Music Awards, hosted that year by Marie Osmond. After a few days of rehearsals, Marie stood on the stage and asked, "Does anyone have any drugs?" Marie had a migraine, and she was looking for some relief. Autumn offered to do trigger point work on her neck, and Marie invited her to her dressing room for the remainder of the week. When the show ended, Marie took out her chequebook and asked Autumn how much she owed her. Marie told Autumn she helped to get her through the week. Naturally, Autumn said, not a thing. K.D. Lang won best artist that year at the awards. I remember the moment, standing in the back beside Anne Murray and K.D. Lang, two of many lesbian's favourites.

Later that year, Autumn worked on a Hockey Hall of Fame awards show and was invited to a private reception. She knew nothing about hockey at the time. She came home with a photo of her standing with the coveted Stanley Cup, her invitation covered with the autographs of many of the greatest hockey players in our history.

We quickly found a solid community at the Metropolitan Community Church and made new friends, some friendships now over thirty years old.

If we wanted to dance, the Chez Moi club opened in Nineteen eighty-four. It was one of the most popular places for women to congregate in Toronto. Dallas Nofall, a popular D.J. at the club, described it as being like Cheers, but gay. It was the first time I saw a woman in a gay club who looked like a movie star. Dallas was vivacious and had an infectious spirit. When I discovered she was from Newfoundland, it made sense, later two of our best friends would be from Newfoundland, salt of the earth, people I gravitate towards.

We found a community of men and women at the Metropolitan Church who became our family. We were Christians, Catholics, Jews, and even agnostics and atheists. We'd all lived through some level of persecution in our own lives and were a supportive community for one another. We were doctors, lawyers, garbage collectors, and teachers. Our common goal was simple, to live our lives quietly and with purpose, not to judge others as we had been judged. On occasion, we'd all go to church retreats out in the country.

Homophobia was still rampant in the eighties, and women had to be careful about flaunting their sexuality. We were accosted on the street by men yelling insults at us and calling us names. We were still very closeted. When I first came out, I wanted to shout it to the world. I felt a sense of freedom I'd never known. One of the first things I did was go to the Women's bookstore and buy myself a shirt proclaiming my preference to the world.

"A woman needs a man like a fish needs a bicycle."

Many of our friends were men, both straight and gay, so it wasn't an inference about men, just the excitement for me, that I was finally going to live my life the way I thought I was meant to live it, with a woman. Whether I had the shirt on or not, men still harassed us daily. Are you dykes or femmes, or just Lezzies?"

*Jamie and Mandy at
English Bay in Vancouver
BC - by Mermaid Rock*

*Jamie and Todd going
fishing.*

Aunt Mary with Mandy.

Mandy and Jamie in New York City

Jamie and Mandy with their
Dad, Edward.

Jamie, as the lone wolf in his treehouse, after his father died.

CHAPTER THIRTEEN

East and West

Eventually we moved back to British Columbia again. We loved both provinces, and my family lived in British Columbia. There is something about being born in the mountains that called me back, and each province offered something very different. In the early nineties Autumn was denied same sex benefits at the Bank of Montreal. Because common law couples were able to get it, she filed a human rights lawsuit against the bank on behalf of me as her spouse. It was a tedious and difficult two-year battle. Barbara Findlay, a well-respected lesbian lawyer came on board towards the end. Autumn secured same sex benefits for us, and all employees at the bank.

Shortly after we returned to British Columbia, I spent an idyllic two weeks at a writing and film retreat, with Press Gang Publishers. The dorm like accommodation was in a wooded area in North Vancouver. It lent itself to a welcome respite for the myriad of writers and film makers from across Canada. There were about twenty of us, a varied lot, and probably about half lesbians. Naturally the lesbians gravitated to one another, and soon it became a lesbian soap opera. Everyone who was single, had their eye on Clare, a gorgeous poet who wore brown cowboy boots. She was the perfect catch for everyone who tried to catch her. She was sullen, brooding and aloof, the qualities lesbian women often portray to show their disinterest, even if they are lying to themselves. It's the lesbian dance that became so familiar. I'm really interested in getting to know you, but I'm afraid I'll be rejected, so I'll be as aloof as possible.

I always watched with interest and thought about all the time these women wasted posturing, rather than reaching out. After much drama, Clare ended up in a two week, not forever relationship that ended when we all went back to reality. There was a writer I clicked with instantly over our love of writing and words. We were serious about our work had numerous things in common. A few of the women were pretentious, and we wanted to make light of their attitudes. One day we decided to go to a thrift store where we purchased matronly looking dresses, making the point that we are not what we wear. We wore them to dinner that night, the women who always presented themselves dressed to impress, weren't amused. We were like a group of schoolgirls let loose.

Metis writer and filmmaker, Maria Campbell, was at the retreat as an instructor. She was an enigma to many of the women because of her serenity and was a beacon of light to the unenlightened. Maria was beautiful and regal, her bright blue eyes a stark contrast to her copper skin. I heard some women discussing her one day in hushed tones.

"I wonder what her secret is, she's so calm and mysterious."

One of her secrets was that she talked less, and listened more, that revelation was lost on many. Maria's book, 'Half breed,' described her early difficult life as a woman caught between two cultures. Maria loved going to Value Village to shop for clothes and when we had free time we would jump into my van. Maria filled bags to take home to her family in Saskatchewan. We both left home at a very young age, we understood simplicity and weren't bothered by silence. One day when we were about to leave Value Village, I noticed my van had a flat tire. I went to get help while she waited with the van. When I returned, Maria the mystery woman, was sitting on the pavement beside my flat tire. She was reading The National Enquirer she'd picked up at the gas station beside Value Village. Her secret? Authentically human, not trying to impress anyone, a trait everyone could aspire to. On the last day I collaborated with another writer on a piece we read at the end. It was a parody about taking yourself too seriously.

CHAPTER FOURTEEN

Truth or Circumstance

We wondered if there was an end to this dusty prairie road. The map clearly showed it as a much better route.

"Are you sure he lives out here?"

Autumn was struggling with the well-worn map, and we were beginning to wonder if we'd made a mistake. The map was nearly ragged, having been folded in so many different places.

I haven't seen a building in over an hour. She was right but I wasn't ready to tell her that. I was having my own doubts. It was July and the heat was relentless. I offered.

"I'm almost certain we're going in the right direction."

The truth is, I didn't have a clue where we were, or where we might end up. Behind our thirty-foot motorhome we were towing our Honda Gold Wing motorcycle. Driving a large vehicle on that narrow gravel road obviously required some forethought, but this wasn't a trip with much planning. After Autumn's parents began to continually harass us at our home in Grand Forks, we made a quick decision to hit the road and head east. My children were old enough at this stage to allow us our geographic freedom. I watched the gas gauge hovering near empty and offered a diversion while I looked for a gas station.

"Why don't you put a Chris Williamson tape in the deck, let's just relax while we try to find the place?"

Soon Chris's voice filled our Motorhome, and we were singing along.

'Wake me up from this dream...I need a little peace of mind, you're flowing like a river, the changer and the changed, sometimes it takes a rainy day just to let you know everything's gonna be all right...'

I'd been waiting for that day for some time now. Not long before we left, another grim reality hit us. Acceptance would never come easy for any of us. I thought about my cousin who couldn't live with being gay. My cousin Paul was a tall, lithe young man, adopted by one of my dad's brothers. The first time I saw him, he was three years old, dancing and twirling around the room.

"Quit making a spectacle of yourself!"

My uncle chided him, and the small boy curled up in a corner by himself. I saw the writing on the wall then, but that was still an era when we kept things to ourselves. We'd lost touch long ago, but we were reunited by my aunt Martha. Her oldest son, my cousin Roger was gay. My aunt was one of the early outspoken supporters for same sex relationships. Roger's preferences were accepted by my uncle Bill, and his mother, Martha. We were at a pride celebration in Vancouver at English Bay, and we were sitting on the grass with Aunt Martha and my cousin Roger. In the distance, Paul is dancing, his frail body towering above everyone else, his arms raised to the sky. He is making a spectacle of himself, as well as he should. There is no one there judging him. The sky is clear and blue, and the sun is shining on us all.

Paul's head is thrown back, and he is the little boy I watched curl up in a corner, an ashamed three-year-old. As many gay and trans people experience, the world was too much for Paul.

These beautiful sensitive souls leave us because their personal pain is unbearable.

The lack of acceptance to live their lives without judgement.

Eventually their pain becomes insurmountable, and Paul ended his life shortly after.

I was deep in memories as we hunted for my uncle's house. For a reason I couldn't quite fathom, this meeting with my uncle, my mother's brother, was an important one. The last time I'd seen him I was ten. He'd met me at the train station on horseback. We picked wild berries, watched for the bears, saw eagles swoop over downed deer, and basked in the quiet of the Selkirk Mountains, my birthplace. Eventually, we found a gas station, and since everyone in this Alberta County appeared to be connected, they knew my uncle and directed us to his place. Our week went by quickly and my uncle was the perfect host except for his regular breakfast call.

"It's daylight in the swamp, you're missing the best part of the morning."

The sun would be just peeking up behind the hills, and the welcome aroma of fresh coffee was welcoming. Autumn and I played cards with my uncle and a friend, looked at old photographs, and talked about his life with my mother on their homestead. He didn't want us to leave, and we promised to write until we met again. My uncle and his close male friend would come over to play cards with us in the evenings.

The last evening, we spent sitting on the back porch. We were quietly reminiscing about this peaceful visit, wishing we could stay longer. A prairie storm had broken across the late afternoon sky, and the sunset went suddenly from deep orange to Hyacinth red. There was a certain peace in this place we were in, and words weren't always necessary. My uncle's words flew at me from out of nowhere.

"I don't suppose anyone's told you the truth."

My body froze and his words stuck in my head, while I waited.

His words cut through the colours in the sky. They broke through the hum of the crickets in the distance.

"There wasn't much to you."

He stopped for a minute and picked up his rifle. My gut relaxed and my breathing returned. I knew this story, it was safe. I'd heard many times before how my grandfather helped to deliver me in the log house beside the Fraser River. How I weighed about three pounds, was warmed on the oven door of the cook stove. How my mother wondered if I would survive. My uncle took a red handkerchief from his shirt pocket and ran it over the barrel of the gun. He stood up and pointed it towards the cornfields where the birds were beginning to carouse the tall stalks.

"Of course, we didn't expect you to be much of anything."

The birds weren't frightened by the stuffed scarecrows with their straw arms reaching up to the sky. The crack of the gun broke through the layers of heat built up from the summer prairie storm.

"The way she went at it, trying to get rid of you."

The crows flew off in all directions flying for their lives while my uncle was slipping another round of ammunition into the cartridge. I thought about my mother and our strained relationship throughout the years. The words my father threatened her with when I was three, the words that were always in the back of my mind.

"I'm going to tell her what you did."

Later, the words that would follow me into adulthood.

"I wonder if you are the way you are because..."

Words that made me question myself. Those words finally made sense to me. The way I was, was alive, I'd beat the odds of toxic liquids, falls, and wire coat hangers meant to prevent my birth. I thought about my mother and her lifetime of regret. I knew I played a part in it, and this was a small piece of the puzzle. My body didn't move, and a deep pain gnawed its way to my womb.

"I have feeders all over, but these damn birds just want my corn." My uncle was placing his gun beside the screen door.

"Just thought I'd let you know. You don't owe anyone a damn thing."

With that, he mumbled about having to do something inside. Truth or circumstance, I knew that I got my inner strength for survival from my mother. It didn't matter, I was alive. I didn't need to know any more.

A few months later, on a bitterly cold January day in Toronto, we stood with a group of women outside the Morgentaler abortion clinic. Beside us, the pro-lifers were raucous and persistent, waving their placards in our direction.

"Murderers, murderers, you'll all burn in hell!"

Their words appeared to freeze in mid-air as they met the harsh winter wind.

"Killers of innocent babies!"

A very poor artist thrust a crude picture of a fetus in my face. I turned away from the tormented grimaces. I pulled all my fragmented thoughts together. The protesters tried to prevent a woman from entering the clinic and we went to her aid. I moved in slow motion, from the past to the present, two parts of me merging. I was, at once, where I began, and who I am.

By Chance

The face of my mother is carved

 in stones we gathered on the CN line,

My past, hidden in the shadows of the looming Selkirks.

Ghosts of long gone, school children

abandoned schoolhouses, fifty feet from the Fraser.

I stand quietly

in reverence to my mothers' memories.

rotting wood, remnants of a life long passed, jagged pieces of
our history.

A lone willow spreads branches over the remnants of a house,
protecting the origins of my birth,

I watch my mother as she tries to remember and tries to for-
get.

The spaces between us are vast, her constant innocence as-
tounds me,

I am aware I did not inherit it.

Words separate us, they are sharp and pointed, foul smelling
liquids, crude wire hangers, futile falls.

We are here to reclaim her past, my existence,

by chance.

CHAPTER FIFTEEN

The Long Road Home

As I viewed the photographs more closely, I could see the distance between my mother and me. She never leaned towards me, always away. Although I have my arm around her shoulders, the pain between us shows in our stance. This journey, too, was important. I wanted it for our memories, and to forge a new connection. It was the place her childhood memories were embedded in, where she'd met a man she loved, and lost. It was my birthplace. It wasn't difficult to persuade her to visit her old homestead, but I don't think she was prepared for the ghosts of her past. A diminutive woman from hardy stock, not five feet tall, she always prided herself on her independence. Those of us who knew her well didn't always agree with that stance. Her time was allotted to either dealing with the needs she felt obliged to fulfill or worrying about how she would find time to fulfill them.

I made note of her constant patter as we continued along rutted roads; she mumbled a lot, and I constantly asked her to speak up. This annoyed her, and she had a habit of pretending she hadn't really said anything, or at least anything worth repeating. She'd replace it with something mundane and insignificant.

"Do you see that hawk swooping over the field, must be a downed deer."

She would peer out the car window as if her life depended on clarifying her hunch. Soon we were at a verbal impasse again, and I wondered when we stopped having meaningful conversations, or if we ever had them. I was mulling this over when she dangled a carrot, recounting a story about me when I was three, before we moved to the city.

"I was so damned scared, one minute you were playing in front of the house, and the next you were gone."

She had told this story before, and I waited patiently for the part about the bears, so I could shake my head appropriately. As we physically approached the place where it had happened, an old story gathered new life.

"I was calling you and couldn't find you anywhere, I thought the bears had you. I ran down the road and there you were, watching your uncle fix the fence."

She started to say,

"You sure were an independent little..."

But her voice trailed off. Silence grew between us, as we had reached our biggest point of contention. Her life, full of service and dedication, with no freedom to exist without being controlled, and my life, a universe away and full of all the possibilities that were closed off to her. She would groan and move about on the car seat. We asked if she would like to stop and stretch her legs, but she denied her discomfort. I knew that her pattern was to suffer, so we stopped anyway. My mother gazed at the Selkirk Mountains, and told us that she remembered during the war, they had a lookout up there. She closed her lips over a cigarette and inhaled, a habit she kept forever, one that had almost ended her life a few years before. When we resumed our drive, I was privy to the nicotine residue. I had learned to endure this silently because she was my only mother.

The last roads we came across had ruts a foot deep. Until the nineties the only access to this remote place was by plane, boat or train. We drove the car gingerly between the ruts, trying to discern if the left or the right, was more manageable. We finally pulled up to the gate, which enclosed the vast expanse of land that knew the secrets of my mother's youth. The gate was closed, and there were warning signs plastered everywhere. My mother, in her usual fashion, pretended they did not exist as she flung open the gate and flagged me through. She rationalised with no one in particular, the way she felt about her child-hood home.

"When you own a place for almost a century it always feels like yours."

Just five years earlier, the homestead had changed hands when my uncle died.

"For Christ's sake you'd think they could clean up the yard!"

My mother said this because the owners were strangers living on her land. The yard was about two hundred acres and had all the trappings of a farm. A vicious dog threatened to rip our throats open if we came any closer.

"Shut up!"

My mother threatened him right back. "I said go lie down, get out of here!"

She shook her small arthritic hand at him.

"Jesus, I hate dogs barking like that for no reason."

I was not going to remind her that we were on the dog's property. She pointed to somewhere in the distance, and I could read the pain in her eyes as she remembered what had long passed, with no chance of it happening again.

"Down there, that's where I used to set traps with my father."

Her arm swept through the air, to a place long gone. She pulled anoth-
er cigarette from her pack and lit it while she stared off into another
distant memory.

"That is where you were born."

She was pointing to an open field. My heart thumped as I thought of
my tenuous fight to survive inside her womb. In the distance, a lone
willow tree spread its branches protectively over the remains of a log
house. All that was left of my birthplace was old wood, rotting and
broken. We made our way down, walking on a path a stone's throw
from the Fraser River. The wind was howling loudly, and I could only
catch pieces of her conversation. She told me again that two of her
brothers had drowned in that river. I knew that, but this was the day
we would recall those events in the place they happened. My mother
moved her arm up into the air again.

"I could stand right under his arm."

She was talking about Ernest, her twin, the second one to fall victim to
the whirling waters. She switched subjects smoothly before any emo-
tion could surface, pointing to another empty field.

"That's where the old schoolhouse was."

The vacant desolate spot gave no indication that happy children ever
inhabited it, but I stood quietly in respect for her childhood memories.
She shifted memories quickly.

"Everyone was sure scared the night you were born."

She took a long drag from her cigarette, staring into the distance. We'd
never spoken about her numerous attempts to abort me.

"Were you scared, I asked tentatively."

She almost spit out her reply. She rolled her faded brown eyes at me.

"For Christ's sake, I was only having a baby."

We did not pursue this. Everything that came easy for her, including childbirth was the opposite for me.

"You were born in a matter of minutes, just before the midnight train whistle blew, we never knew if the clocks were right, it was either the 14th or the 15th."

From the field that once buzzed with the activity of schoolchildren, and the laughter of long-gone siblings, we wound our way back. Driving slowly along the dusty road in search of the cemetery, my mother caught sight of an elderly woman. She was standing in front of an official post office, the size of an outdoor toilet. My mother rolled down her window and gave a holler.

"Is that you, Terese?"

Aside, she said to me.

"Jesus, it's old lady McCoy, I thought she'd be dead."

Nostalgia permeated my senses, while I sat in old lady McCoy's kitchen. Johnny Cash blared from the radio.

'Down, down, down, and the flames went higher, the ring of fire.'

My mother and the friend from her youth exchanged small talk. I feasted my eyes on a kitchen that had not been updated since the thirties. My mother was peering around the room.

"Do you still have that old gramophone?"   "Nope," old lady McCoy answered flatly.

"You don't? Well, what happened to it?"

My mother was almost confrontational, and old lady McCoy's head shook slightly, as she peered at my mother, with the suspicion of an old school friend, you weren't sure you could trust.

They looked at photographs of their children, some more than half a century old. Old lady McCoy seemed to be obsessed with the height of my older brother.

"Oh, he's sure big, eh?

Every comment ended with, eh?

"He was in love with that Carol girl, I remember. They were lovey-dovey, eh. Yeah, he sure got to be a big man, eh?"

She looked over at my mother, and back at the photograph.

"You sure look small beside him, eh?"

My mother looked small beside many people. She lit up another cigarette and blew out a long line of smoke. She didn't answer. This journey to her past seemed to be overwhelming her. After a silence she asked her old friend another question.

"I see it's all grown over where the mill used to be, what happened?" She did not wait for an answer.

"So what about the graveyard, I suppose it's all grown over too?"

I stared at the yellow and black tiles covering the bottom half of the kitchen wall and thumbed through a Watkins cookbook older than my mother.

"Yes, it is, pretty well."

Old lady McCoy's headshake continued slightly when she spoke.

"Why don't they clean it up?"

My mother demanded to know, even if was decades since she'd lived here, and no longer had claim to this land.

Old lady McCoy explained that the Canadian National owned the property, and they were waiting for some papers so they could turn it over to the community.

"They're supposed to give us a one-thousand-dollar grant to do it."

I managed to suppress a smile. Away out here in the middle of nowhere, the word 'grant' sounded out of place. My mother almost sputtered,

"Well, for God's sake, you have people buried there, don't you?"

My mother told us that she used to run like hell past the cemetery when she was young. Later we made a quick stop there, where the headstone of another of her brothers led the way into dense bush. She stood and read the inscription.

"Here lies a son and brother, March is a windy month."

My mother was upset that she couldn't find the grave of her grandmother, everything was now covered in rotting trees, and dense bush.

We walked along the railroad tracks and gathered rocks together, while she told me stories I'd never heard before, one of them about my father throwing my baby brother in the river. My mother spotted a bear and got excited, the thrill of hunting still in her blood.

"Jeez, I wish I had my gun."

I winced, remembering the close calls she had had being chased by that moose, and other escapades.

I felt a sense of loss as we left this place, I knew my mother and I would probably never walk the path of her childhood together again. Clearly, she was still a pioneer, and I was a daughter who did not follow in her footsteps. Along the way she spotted chokecherries, and we stopped to pick them. She was relaxed and looking for berries, while I was worried about the wildlife that lived in the bushes. As a child I never worried about bears, but when I became a city dweller that all changed.

"What about the bears?"

"Don't worry about bears, we'll scare them off."

She waved her hand in the air again, as confident in the wilderness as I am in the city. When we left, we drove alongside the train tracks. My mother stopped again for her last cigarette before the journey home. The pain of remembering was clear on her face, the once youthful young woman she was back then, vanished, she was a warrior of a difficult life long lived. I watched her silently remembering her past, the ghosts all around her. The train station where her lover left her and went off to war was gone. The train that carried hopeful lovers, and sometimes dead babies and children was part of her past. Not surprisingly, it was one of her last thoughts on this journey.

"I'd sure like to see a train on these tracks one more time before we go."

Almost before she finished speaking, the CN train came around the bend, three lights catching the sunlight, with a long mournful whistle. This sound was the lullaby of my mother's childhood. We watched it wind through the landscape, and as the train disappeared around the corner my mother dropped her cigarette, ground it into the dirt with her shoe, and looked up at me.

"That's enough."

CHAPTER SIXTEEN

A New Beginning

It took thirty years for my mom to leave my abusive father. With so many children to care for, twelve over a span of two decades, and no control over her finances, she was beaten down by circumstance. Her two youngest were nine and eleven when she made the final break. My father's frustration and anger rose to a crescendo when he lost control. Suddenly it was important for him to see his kids. After all those years of, stay the hell out of my way!

"They're my kids, and I want to see them."

He'd been harassing my mom after she left, even from hundreds of miles away. I'd stopped by to visit her when he called. Once again, she was at his mercy.

"They're in school, and I don't know how you expect me to do that, there's eight hundred miles between us."

Yes, thankfully, I thought to myself.

My mom was still trying to appease him. I remember him calling out my mom for swearing many years ago, but he gave her a run for her money this time, and I could hear his angry voice through the phone. I watched my mother's face tense up. She was back in that place where he had her down on the floor, ripping out her hair, before he knocked her teeth out. She looked helpless again, not the strong woman who laboured alongside her father, or the independent woman who worked on warships, hot rivets barely missing her eye.

Not the woman who could handle a gun like Annie Oakley, and shoot bears and moose. Not the girl who set traps alongside her father.

"You think you can keep those kids from me, I'll show you."

I watched him break her down, word by word. When she spoke again, she was meek, her voice barely above a whisper.

At that point, I grabbed the phone from her.

"Who do you think you are?" I yelled into the receiver.

He was startled.

"Who is this?"

"Your daughter and I'm not afraid of you, leave my mother alone or I'll call the police."

I hung up, my mother and I both shaking. She stood there like a whipped dog, chewing her lip. He wasn't her first choice, the man she wanted to spend her life with was someone else, and he never forgot that. This was her lifelong punishment, a cruel marriage that ensured the safekeeping of the child she had with her lover, and a dream that ended before it began. The laws supported men, not the women they impregnated.

Once he heard me blurt out my challenge, he left her alone.

I was, as my mother always said, "a tenacious little shit."

As a child he made me pay for my freedom in other ways. Belt buckles until my legs were welted and bleeding, whips and steel-toed boots. A child who would grow up afraid to speak or breath. A child searching for a way out of her life, from an early age.

My mother had broken away, but her transition into freedom wasn't easy. She didn't know how to handle money, and the little she was given in her divorce settlement was quickly squandered. There were constant family dramas unfolding and she was always in the middle of them. Around the same time, my sister's fiancé was killed in a boating accident and my mom's youngest brother died in a car accident. I don't know if it was resilience or resignation that kept her going. I watched while others fell apart, and my mother showed little emotion. I'd only heard her cry once in my life, just before my brother Paddy passed away.

While my mother was experiencing her first few years of freedom from her marriage, I was about six years into mine with Edward. Her years of subservience to my father had taken their toll. I couldn't tell her I was unhappy. As far as she was concerned, I was lucky that a wonderful man had married me. Over the next few years after I moved to Toronto, we wrote letters and talked on the phone. I didn't acknowledge it at the time, but I'd buried my past deep inside my body where I couldn't reach it. I fooled myself into thinking that my early lifetime of trauma had no effect on who I was now. Like my mother, I was adept at diverting attention away from my needs. I entered a world where I thought I might fit in, but I was still unsure, watching and observing, picking up cues. On the outside I appeared to have it together. A born mimic, I could dress and act the part I needed to play; inside I was terrified, still unable to breathe freely.

My father was like a volcano, quiet and almost non-existent until the next eruption. We had no idea what would set him off or when it would occur. He kept all of us waiting. The unknown was wreaking damage on my body and my mind long before I left home. It took another sixty years before the trauma surfaced and I was able to find peace. There were many moments of joy along the way, the birth of my children and grandchildren, my relationship with Autumn, my life partner of thirty-five years. I still jumped at loud noises, felt my body going into flight mode in a flash. I thought if I was strong, I would be able to let it all go. I was wrong.

Although we were often separated by geography, my mother's history stayed with me. Looking back, I could see cues that would evoke emotion, just as quickly, as I watched how she would suppress them. Parts of her were childlike, her faded brown eyes could sparkle with life at remembering events she cherished. The far away look would take over when the memories were painful. She remained quick witted with a sense of humour to the end. I loved her so thoroughly and silently as I watched her age. Eventually, she was content to fall asleep on the couch, while younger generations prepared family dinners. Later she'd be fast asleep, her Dick Franpocketbookbook, rising and falling on her chest. My childhood was immersed with her pain, but along with what she couldn't give me, there were lifelong lessons. The empathy and compassion she showed for others, along with her generosity were instilled into me early.

Observing my small childhood world in silence, also opened a world of awareness.

Valuable lessons can evolve from emotional isolation. I tried to see life through her eyes during her last years. When I was a four-year-old, there wasn't much to look back on, but I thought endlessly about who my mother might have been, as a child like me. Living with despair over events I had no control over was bred into me.

"We could all be blown to bits, tomorrow might not come, we could die in our sleep."

There was no limit to the number of disasters my mother could conjure up. I knew she was going to die one day, and I began to prepare for it over the last decade of her life. She would linger at her screen door after a visit. Looking back, I wished we'd stayed for another hand of crib, and wandered around in her garden with her pointing out how large the rhubarb had grown. We were in a good place before she left us. I told her again that I didn't do funerals, and I didn't want hers to be my last memory of us together. I noticed small things about her more. She rarely completed a thought if an emotion surfaced, and her animation at recalling a painful event or memory would stop abruptly. I could always read her pain in remembering. If a headline read, by the year 2020.... she would flick off the news.

"I'll be long dead by then."

There was no arguing the fact. We all have questions and what ifs. Most are futile when examining our pasts. What was, is the hand you were dealt. You survived. The story grows from there. I wouldn't change much of my life, and every day I wake up with gratitude. Like my mother before me, I learned to make the best of what I was given, finding beauty in simplicity. Most days I wake up and kiss the sun. There is gratitude that my mother's coat hangers didn't reach me. Gratitude she was able to paint my tiny fingernails to match my first birthday dress.

My mother's penchant for making sure everyone else's comfort came before hers was a trait I inherited. A degree in Social Work was probably the last profession for me. Even before I received my degree from the University of Victoria, I was trying to save the world. My formal quest began at Lenore Walker's first International Conference on battered woman, at the University of Alberta. From there, I ferried terrified women and frightened children to safe houses, hiding them from violent spouses. Securing safe housing for women attempting to leave violent relationships, on the Blood reserve in Alberta, and spending his last days with a violent sex offender before I quit my position at the ministry. The last straw, working with a mother and her son. An innocent child, lost to his mother at seven, for reasons of economics and religion, I was done with a system I no longer had faith in.

My mother was every woman I tried to save, and I was every frightened child. Now I know we play house all our lives. We can't deny the connectedness of our past, present and future.

Like a vinyl record on an antique phonograph, we go round and round. My mother and I, connected by a tenuous fibre of our being in utero and throughout our lives.

"Ubuntu", a Zulu philosophy, describes us perfectly, "I am because you are."

*Mandy and Lorne Green making a
commercial together.*

*Mandy in front of the St Lawerence
Centre in Toronto when she was in Six
Characters.*

Mandy as Helen Keller in the Miracle Worker at YPT (Young People's Theatre) in Toronto.

Mandy in Six Characters in Search of an Author with Denise Assante - Toronto, Ontario.

Mandy auditioning for Annie in New York.

CHAPTER SEVENTEEN

Before and After

"The fucking bitch did it on purpose, it was road rage."

The next thing I remember is a large man, his face contorted in anger. He was pounding furiously on the window of my motor home, inches from my face, screaming at me.

"Open the window, open this fucking window."

Our three-year-old grandson was sitting on the seat beside me. He'd been fast asleep before the incident. He woke up with a start, his dark ringlets stuck to the side of his head from the relentless heat and humidity. His frantic words would remain in my ears.

"Are people dead, are people dead?"

In a matter of moments my life became, 'before' and 'after,' the accident.

Earlier in the day, the band in the July 1st parade had sent cheerful vibrations from Osoyoos out over the Okanagan. We watched the small-town parade, then headed down to the park. An assortment of vendors had set themselves up at display tables and food trucks. My mother enjoyed the parade, but the relentless desert heat was getting to her, and she asked me to take her back home. She was still recovering from her carotid artery surgery only weeks before. She was living in happy isolation on top of Anarchist Mountain nearby. It was about twenty minutes away from the town, a long climb past the top of the summit.

I took her home in my van, and then drove my thirty-foot motor home back down, so she could have comfort when she returned later. The over three-thousand-foot panorama from the Anarchist Summit back down to the town of Osoyoos is breathtaking. The highway winds and snakes down the mountain. A lookout halfway down, allows a sweeping view of the city, lakes and mountains below, and across the valley. The forty-degree heat was rising from the hills, dotted with prickly sagebrush and a few jack pines that had survived the latest forest fire. The small town appeared at the bottom of the winding highway. Osoyoos has one of Canada's most endangered ecosystems and is one of the hottest places in the country. The descent from the high elevation has frightened visitors who aren't accustomed to some of British Columbia's Mountain roads. With my mother perched on top of the mountain, I knew this highway in every season like the back of my hand. The crowds had intensified while I was gone as I made my way carefully down the knoll.

To my left, a woman was standing beside her vendor booth, a hand on her car door. As a proficient and seasoned motor home driver, I understand the amount of space necessary to manoeuvre a rig this size. I'd driven my motor home through traffic in Los Angeles, Las Vegas, Chicago, down to New Mexico and California. I'd driven it across Canada, and the United States a dozen times over the years. I watched for a few seconds wondering if the woman was planning to drive out. If she was, I'd need to wait to park, or I would block her.

"Do you need to get out?"

I ran about ten feet to ask if she needed to exit. No, she said, she thought she'd stay put. The traffic in the area was intense. Straight ahead there was a small city bandshell, to the right, a beer garden, and around the park vendors on either side. About three minutes had passed since I'd arrived. After my brief conversation with the woman beside her car, I slid back into my motor home, my grandson sound asleep. What happened next would spiral me into two years of hell, and make me question the feasibility of trust, the media, and especially our legal system. The last thing I remember is shifting my motor home into drive, preparing to only move forward a few feet and pull close to the curb. Within seconds it shot towards the bandshell, crashing into a parked van. The steering wheel was violently jerked from my hands on impact, and the motor home struck three vehicles and seven people, as it catapulted through the crowds between the vendors. Someone said a tire was thrown that stopped the motor home. I don't remember. I was sitting in the middle of the angry crowd in shock. I could barely speak when the pounding began at my window. I do remember calmly rolling it down, as if this were a bad dream. An angry man screamed and swore at me, inciting the crowd. I found out later he was a retired police officer. The high-pitched sounds of police cars, fire trucks, and ambulances filled the air. There were faces everywhere staring at us, shouting obscenities. The police opened my motor home door, came in and closed it, and asked what happened?

"I don't know, it just took off."

No one died, but there were significant serious injuries and the motor home had destroyed three vehicles in its path. An angry biker came to my window to verbally assault me.

"You fucking bitch, you destroyed my Harley."

I was incredulous that people could think that anyone who was of sound mind would set out on such a beautiful day, grandchild in tow, to destroy lives, including my own. No one asked me how we were, or if we needed anything. I'd already been convicted by the public.

I couldn't even begin to explain the scene. Angry people yelling and screaming, the injured were being put into ambulances, destroyed vehicles lying around us. I held my grandson in my arms, the familiar odour from his damp hair, a comfort.

Around that time, the TV show, 'Dateline,' had released information about serious problems with Ford 150 engines. Numerous accidents and deaths had recently resulted from sudden acceleration. It was the same engine as my motor home. I did hours of research on this, reading horror stories, like mine. When I presented the information to my first lawyer, he printed it out, and charged me thousands of dollars, before he told me.

"None of this is admissible in court."

It made sense. I wondered why this information wasn't available to everyone.

"ROAD RAGE, WOMAN PLOWS THROUGH CROWD."

I woke up to that headline on the front page of one of Canada's major newspapers the following day. There were dozens of stories about who I was, and where I'd been. There was no mention of the fact that I was at a family event, had grandchildren with me, just a crazy woman hellbent on destruction. I was reluctant to go out in public. A large photo of my motor home displayed on the front page, my young grandson and I, somewhere inside. There were hundreds of angry people milling around; we were like two frightened animals in a cage. My nine-year-old granddaughter was standing a few feet away from the path of the motor home as it careened through the crowds. If she hadn't been scooped up by my niece standing beside her, she might have been run over too. She told me years later.

"I remember a cloud of dust being picked up quickly, and watching people throw rocks at our motor home, people screaming at you, and I was crying."

The accident had repercussions that were long and far-reaching, I lost two years of my life in fear I was going to prison. The fact that these engines were causing accidents from unexplained sudden acceleration was lost on the legal system. They were only interested in finding reasons to convict me to appease the public's anger. Three months later, in early October, I was dropping my grandson off at preschool when one of the mothers approached me, stopping by my car window.

"I heard on CBC Radio this morning that you have seven criminal charges against you." When I got home, I called my lawyer and fired him. I foolishly thought it would all go away. I was a grandmother, three of my grandchildren were with me the day of the accident. But none of those facts mattered to our antiquated legal system. I soon learned that the system is like a chess game, two opposing sides, Crown counsel and my lawyer, trying to outdo one another. Truth had little to do with it. After I was formally charged, I sought out another lawyer. This one only took a couple of thousand dollars from me, before I understood he was useless. I finally found not only a phenomenal lawyer, but a human being above reproach.

Paul Danyliu reminded me of the title character in Colombo at our first meeting. Rumpled and constantly smoking, he was a renowned and I respected criminal lawyer with decades of experience. He was legendary for his skills in the examination of witnesses. I'd spoken to him briefly on the phone. His expertise was primarily in high profile murder and drug cases, but Paul was curious enough about my case to agree to meet with me. I soon discovered that he believed in truth and justice above all, it wasn't just about winning.

Paul's desk was piled high with clutter, and there were papers strewn everywhere. I watched his cigarette ash fall, and he quickly brushed it off his desk. He bumbled about silently arranging his papers. I watched him making his moves, and I could sense that we were both evaluating the possibility of working together. I liked him immediately. His crumpled suit jacket, his dark brooding good looks, and the quiet before he spoke. I knew he was the one. When I explained the accident and the charges, he agreed that it shouldn't have gone this far. None of the twenty-seven witnesses were proven to be credible. It was a case of crowd hysteria. I wasn't the type of client he usually bothered with, but the Crown was out to lynch me, a fifty-four-year-old woman who had never been on the wrong side of the law. He agreed to represent me, and I knew I was in excellent hands.

The Preliminary Inquiry wasn't as sensational as people hoped, given that the accident had been the talk of the town for months. I was in a gas station on my way to Vancouver while waiting for the trial and heard two customers talking to the cashier.

"We heard she came driving down that road a hundred miles an hour, and she purposely drove her motor home into the crowd."

In fact, I was stopped and in park before my motor home accelerated. Later, when Paul Danyliu and I went down and measured the distance, there was only 30 feet, the entire length of my motor home, between where I started, and the site of the first impact.

The Inquiry was a bad joke, with only about ten people in the courthouse. The witnesses were asked to point to the woman they saw driving the motor home, they all pointed to my sister, ten years younger than me. She has dark hair, and I am blonde. One witness said she saw me in the bar above the park before the accident. Another swore that I was angry and having an argument with my husband, who was sitting in the passenger seat of the motor home. Yet another described me as about thirty, with glasses and short curly hair. The witness accounts were laughable. No one saw me, except for the woman I had spoken to prior to getting back into my motor home. After the Inquiry, Paul was sure the Crown would drop it. There was no motive, no substantial evidence, and no witness accounts to lay charges against me. We were both shocked when they decided to proceed with a trial. Paul said I was being tried in the court of public outrage.

There were seven criminal charges against me, dangerous driving causing bodily harm. Looking at similar cases, I was facing ten years in prison at worst, or house arrest with a bracelet at best, if convicted. My community wrote letters on my behalf. Doctors and teachers whose children were friends with my grandchildren, teachers I'd helped when I'd volunteered on numerous field trips and in classrooms, music teachers who'd taught my grandchildren. None of these statements mattered to Crown Counsel. They were only there to win. I knew I had one of the brightest and best lawyers in the country on my side, but I felt beaten down by a legal system that focused on sensationalism instead of the truth.

Paul and I began preparing for my trial. It had been scheduled for an entire week, ending on Friday December 13th. We met every morning to look at my case over breakfast while we made decisions together on how to proceed. We developed a wonderful working relationship and a comfort with one another. He brought his court jacket for me to replace a button, the night before the trial. Unlike many lawyers, Paul involved me in every step along the way. Initially, he wanted to bring up my early years and my difficult youth. I flatly refused.

"This isn't about my childhood, it's about what happened, telling the absolute truth of what occurred."

I wanted to tell the truth, not make up an excuse for something out of my control. He allowed me to do it my way. I didn't think that having a judge pity me for my childhood, had anything to do My future was in the hands of people who didn't know me. I was only a number. At the trial, there was one other witness who had viewed the accident up close. In fact, very close. She gave a true account of the sudden acceleration. Her account of what she saw was a gift to me. She told the court exactly what happened.

"I was checking myself out in the side mirror on the passenger side of the motor home. In a flash, it accelerated at a high speed, and just took off. I could see the driver's face, and she looked terrified."

The judge asked her to describe me at that moment.

"Like a cat about to be thrown into the lake."

Anyone who has driven a motor home that size would know that they don't normally accelerate that quickly, or at that speed. No expert ever visited that fact. I elected trial by judge, which turned out to be the right choice. The judge was a kind older man who'd probably heard it all. I testified on my own behalf at the end. It was a decision Paul wasn't initially certain about, but again I questioned him as to how they could not believe the truth. I just stood there and told the judge what happened. I was beyond being nervous by this time. I'd already spent the past two years concerned about what my life would look like if I was convicted. The thought of losing my freedom was as dire as death. In the end, the judge acquitted me and paid me a gracious compliment after listening to the testimonies of my personal witnesses.

"You've been an example in your life, of what we could all strive for."

The trial took an emotional and physical toll on me. It lasted a full week, and every day there were TV cameras and news media hanging around outside after a long day in court. I was featured on the evening news every night. There were six witnesses who testified on behalf of my character, including a close friend who was a member of the RCMP, Tom Erickson. Another long-time friend, Jean Pinto, talked about the time I gave to the community, videotaping events for children and their parents. A local teacher and doctor wrote me character references.

Jean was a pillar of the community, and along with her partner Liz, she taught music. They ran a highly successful drama program for children for about twenty years. Four of my grandchildren were fortunate to be their students.

My daughter was nine months pregnant when she gave her testimony, the last one before I took the stand.

"She's been a wonderful mother, our dad died when I was eleven, she's an incredible grandmother, and would never see harm come to her grandchildren, or any child. For years she's videotaped plays, recitals, sports events for her own grandchildren and many others in the community."

The trial ended in my favour, but there had already been extensive damage to my health during the two years I lived in a nightmare.

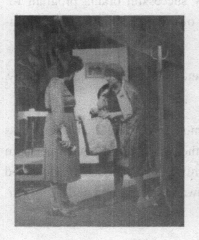

Megan (Eve) in "Waiting for the Parade."

Hushed the movie - based on Megan Hutton's Play Hush.

Megan's Play Committed to Maybe (with Samantha Lazon) Alumnae Theatre Toronto Ontario

A best female film award for Hushed at the Virgin Springs Cinefest, Kolkata India.

The cast of Megan's Play Euchred at Alumnae Theatre
Toronto Ontario.

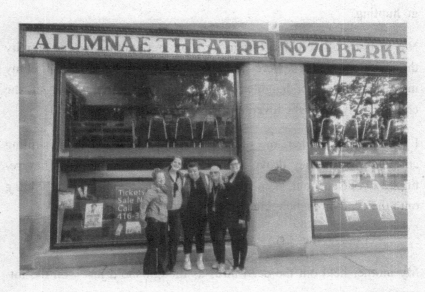

Megan and Cast of Hush the Play at Alumnae Theatre
Toronto Ontario.

CHAPTER EIGHTEEN

Saying Goodbye

As I aged alongside my mother, it was evident she was slowing down. She kept many physical discomforts to herself. My mom was still up for new adventures. She had many interests in common with my partner Autumn. They'd developed a close bond over the years. My mother loved the crack of a gun, and hunting. Any opportunity to get out into the bush brought her pleasure.

"There must be dozens of grouse in those hills, how about we go hunting?"

Not that any of us had to forage for food, but hunting was an activity they both enjoyed and were skilled at. With my partner in her life, my mom had the perfect daughter. Autumn had no children to babysit, she could fix anything, she loved to hunt, and she rode a motorcycle.

I watched my mother, the pioneer woman, and my partner, smiling and chatting, as they drove away in our car, rifles in tow. They returned about an hour later, dead birds in hand, both at ease holding onto the dead birds, hanging by their necks.

"Look at these, now we need to cook them up for dinner."

My mother held out the dead birds as though she'd just won the lottery.

I went into the house while the two of them took the birds into the backyard and skinned them.

A few days later, she was just as excited about a ride on our touring bike, a Honda Gold Wing.

She spoke in that soft voice she used when she wasn't sure if she was deserving.

"Autumn, do you think you could take me for a ride on the bike?"

She was well into her seventies now and had lived with severe heart disease for years. A sideways smile would always accompany her requests. In many ways she reminded me of a small child asking for a treat she wasn't sure she would get. Autumn took my silver helmet, adjusted it on my mom's head and showed her how to use the intercom. I laughed.

"You might regret hooking her up to that."

My mom grinned from ear to ear, the helmet squishing her cheeks, my leather jacket folded around her tiny body. She turned around to wave as they roared out of the driveway. My aging mom called to me.

"Maybe we'll just keep going!"

There could have been a hint of truth in those words. She was living a new life, free of responsibility for others, having finally left and divorced my father after thirty years. He lived close by, and they remained civil. There were many grandchildren and great grandchildren in the picture by this time, which helped relieve underlying tensions at family events.

The bike disappeared up the hill and over the summit, and by dusk they were back. My mom was beaming, the smile on her face, spoke volumes.

"That's one of the best days I've had in a long time."

Autumn undid the helmet and lifted it from my mom's head.

"Your mom is a speed demon, she kept asking me to go faster."

We laughed and watched her hands fly up to her head.

"My hair must be a mess."

All those years, with everything she'd lived through, she still worried about her hair and lipstick. We were opposites, me with my flyaway long hair and no cosmetics. Her needs were simple, and she never would risk asking for too much. Eventually, we all called her grandma. She had so many children, grandchildren, and great grandchildren that she became Grandma to everyone who knew her. We were visiting one day with our granddaughter, when the three-year-old started to sing, "You are my Sunshine." My mom was standing at the sink washing her coffee cup. She turned around with her eyes full of tears.

"Do you know this song, Grandma?"

Later, my mother told us that was the song Hugh always sang to her, and her to their son. As time passed, it became more difficult to say goodbye when we left after a visit. We lived about two hours away, and she was alone on top of a mountain with heart problems. One day, as though she was reading my mind, she looked at me with resignation, reading my thoughts.

"I can't live forever, you know."

We both knew that, but these last years had made up for the times we were living far apart. My first granddaughter bore an uncanny resemblance to me as a baby and toddler. One day I watched my mother curling her hair with a curling iron, as though she was reliving the days when she would put mine in rags. With every health scare we had to face my mom's vulnerability. One early evening she called me, almost apologetic.

"I'm feeling funny, but it's probably nothing."

A triple bypass in her fifties had only been the beginning of her cardiovascular issues.

"Describe funny, mom, are you having chest pain?"

There was silence on the other end, she was still last on her list.

"It's probably nothing, like I said."

While my mom loved the isolation of the house on the mountain, we worried about her dying up there on her own. Some of my siblings lived nearby but she was alone in her house.

"I'll be fine, I'll call my doctor tomorrow."

She was quick to negate her needs.

"No mom, we are on our way."

When Autumn and I arrived at the hospital the doctor checked her out immediately.

"It's a good thing you brought her in, she's in congestive heart failure."

She looked so small, vulnerable and relieved, lying in her hospital bed. Autumn and I booked into a hotel nearby until she was ready to come home. The next day when we arrived to visit, the nurses were smiling. She'd already endeared herself to them.

"I guess it's not my time to go, I've got a few years left in me."

The nurses laughed.

"I just don't know what they'll do with you when you get to heaven."

"That's probably not my direction, my mom quipped."

My mom chewed on the licorice all sorts we'd brought her and was released after a couple of days. On the way back to her house, she was back to her old self.

"Can you stop at a store so I can buy cigarettes?"

That was a habit she wasn't about to change. Smoking was her comfort.

Eventually I introduced her to a video camera so I could record her stories. It didn't go well in the beginning.

"Put that bloody thing away."

"It's just a video camera mom, we can erase anything you don't like."

Her hands flew to her hair.

"My hair isn't done, and I need some lipstick."

We began to film her in baby steps, after a while she forgot it was on. I reminded her she'd recently told me she wasn't going to be here forever.

That was as close as we got to acknowledgment of her imminent death. It was always the same, she'd pat her hair and check her lipstick.

"Is my bald spot covered?"

The compact would come out, she'd apply her signature red lipstick, move her lips together, and snap the compact closed.

"Now I don't look like I'm half dead."

We heard many stories about her past she'd never told us before. I recorded her every chance we had. She was an avid card player, and familiar items were a constant on her kitchen table: the crib board, a deck of cards, cigarettes, lighter, a Dick Francis or a Louis l'Amour novel. If she didn't have company to play cards with, she had her books. I was so grateful she'd instilled her love of books and reading in me when I was young. She told us many long-kept secrets, and opinions during those card games that sometimes lasted for a few hours. There were times when my mother would chew on her bottom lip, stare out into space and come up with comments out of the blue.

"I should have known he was a goddamn liar when he told his family the baby was his."

Then she would deal the cards before her next thought.

"He knew we planned to be together when the war was over."

She always referred to the man she'd loved and lost many decades ago with reverence, then resignation.

"I guess it's all water under the bridge now."

She'd deal the cards quickly then watch to see if I was checking the bottom of the deck.

"For Christ's sake, don't look at the bottom card, that's cheating."

My mother went in and out of past and present, as easily as she dealt the cards. A story I'd heard before gathered new life.

"He threw the baby in the river once when he was mad, can you imagine a grown man throwing a baby in a river?"

I didn't remind her that I had lived through my own personal hell with him.

"Oh damn, you wouldn't believe my hand, I have to give you two."

Then she'd lapse into remembering her childhood.

"Did you know my daddy could make anything out of wood?"

When she spoke about her childhood her voice was soft and childlike, without missing a beat she was back in the present.

"Geez, look at that, a Jack, two sixes, a four, and five, beat that!"

We knew better than to look at our own cards until she counted hers.

"Damn, I shouldn't have given you that ten."

Our card games were memorable and precious, one of her greatest pleasures during those last years.

She loved her flowers. Tiny hummingbirds buzzed at the feeders outside her kitchen window. With winter approaching, the feeders were empty, and the morning mist was creeping over the distant hills. Snow was beginning to feather the branches of the massive fir tree in her front yard. She caught us one day with a request, that small smile at the corner of her mouth.

"You know what I'd like for Christmas?"

We waited while she got her words out.

"I'd like to see lights on that fir tree, don't you think that would be pretty?"

Autumn and I exchanged glances. We both knew we'd do anything she asked that made her life more pleasurable. We looked at the tree outside.

"Mom, that tree has to be ninety feet high, I don't know how we'd get lights up there."

She was still looking at the tree.

"I was just thinking about how pretty it would be, with the lights and the snow." The first branches were at least ten feet up. We went outside and stood beside the tree. A neighbour walked by and stopped to talk.

"Mom wants to put lights on this tree for Christmas."

He ran his hand under his chin and shook his head.

Jesus, Mary and Joseph, you'd need a fire engine ladder to get lights up there." We bought her a ceramic tree with tiny twinkling light bulbs instead, a small compensation for one of her final requests. That would turn out to be her last Christmas. Autumn and I arrived early one evening a few days before the holiday to find her distraught and crying.

"I didn't buy all the kids presents this year."

The kids were sixteen grandchildren, and fourteen great-grandchildren. The past year we were concentrating on keeping her alive. I thought about some of the gifts she'd given me. Two tangible ones were a black diamond ring for my 12th birthday, I guess it was the rage then, and later, a gold heart necklace with a space for two photographs. The most precious gift was our trip back to her old homestead, and the place of my birth. Gathering stones with her on the CN train tracks, her recounting events and stories from those days long past, that was a lasting gift.

The week she died we had a business meeting in a neighbouring city. We dropped her birthday present off at my youngest sister's before we left, and I called her the night before she passed away, not knowing it would be the last time we would talk. She thanked us for her gifts.

"I love my blouses, especially the yellow one with the pretty flowers."

Her needs were simple, she could get as much pleasure from new blouses as another could with a new car.

We never saw them on her. We talked on the phone for a while, said, I love you, and hung up.

The following day Autumn and I were at a restaurant when my daughter called.

"Is Autumn with you?"

I told her yes; we were about to eat dinner.

"Grandma died."

It didn't register at first,

"Whose grandma?"

"Your mom, she died about an hour ago at her house."

I hung up dazed. I called my youngest sister whose husband had found my mother. She told me.

"Her dinner was sitting on the kitchen counter, still warm."

"Where is she now?"

"She's lying on her bed she looks like she's sleeping."

My sister told me about my mom's last day.

"She asked me to take her to town, it was strange because she was so full of energy, almost running from store to store like a teenager. Her legs had been bothering her for months."

I could picture my little mother, all four-foot-nine of her, making every day and moment count right up until the end. I couldn't cry, and kept saying to Autumn, my mom is dead. The words were strange, and I was in shock. The reality didn't hit me until I saw her lying on her bed. I knew she couldn't live forever, but nothing prepares us for the loss of our mother. The implications are far reaching, as the oldest girl, I was statistically next in line.

Autumn was holding back her own tears and we tried to keep it together during the two-hour drive to say goodbye.

I already knew I wanted to say my final goodbye to my mom in her home on the mountain. It was the place where we'd made so many memories over the past few years. We arrived to find her lying on the bed. Her body still warm and making noises, as everything was shutting down. It was surreal to think she wasn't going to wake up and want to play a game of crib. Her Dick Francis novel was folded to page 19 on her bedside table. I leaned over, kissed her on the lips, said, "I love you, mom," for the last time. This time she didn't say,

"I can't live forever, you know."

On my way out, I spotted the plate hanging on her kitchen wall I'd given her for Mother's Day when I was ten. She hung it on her wall wherever she lived, for as long as I could remember. It was white with a scalloped edge, tiny pink and green flowers above, "The Lord's Prayer." I remembered collecting glass milk bottles to pay for it. My mother had chosen her final resting place months before. It was high on a hill, overlooking beautiful Okanagan Lake. For the funeral I would not attend, I made a picture board and asked my daughter to read a short story I'd written. The story I wrote was about the trip that Autumn and I made with my mom to her childhood home a few years back. I was so excited when I gave the book to my mother. After she read it, she had a strange look on her face and was silent. I was disappointed and confused.

"What's wrong mom, don't you like it?"

"It's ok, I guess."

Her response was puzzling at the time, but later I imagined it might be difficult for her to see that part of her life captured in print on a page. She was from the era where we kept our lives private.   The day she was buried, Autumn and I were driving to Toronto. It was Thanksgiving Day, and the fall leaves were vibrant, the colourful trees lining the highway. The clouds were spread across the vast sky, light shining through at intervals, almost coaxing me to believe in heaven. Later, when I saw a photo of my mom in her casket, she was wearing her blue dress, the only one she'd ever owned. The dress was reserved for weddings and funerals. My little mother, Grandma to all who knew her, she'd read her last chapter and put away her cards.

CHAPTER NINETEEN

Finding Jane

I was taught the past was to be left alone. Throughout my life I had difficulty settling. Whether I changed houses or moved across the country I carted my past with me. The many years of being hard-wired for disaster were in my bones, and they caught up with me when I hit my sixties. My anxiety reached a new level when Autumn was misdiagnosed with a rare and terminal carcinoma. After an almost perfect Christmas and New Year's in Toronto, the call from an oncologist gutted both of us. An MRI for headaches prior to Christmas, showed a suspicious mass. I waited for her to arrive home from work after we heard the news, and I stared bleakly at all the things I thought I'd never be able to look at the same way again. The Christmas tree was still up for Ukrainian Christmas. In a trance-like state I began to remove the decorations. Over the next month Autumn endured numerous tests and visits to the cancer hospital. We couldn't talk about it, it was too big. I cried day and night, my pain at the thought of losing her overwhelming. She was angry when I showed emotion and began to push me away.

"I'm the one who is supposed to die."

Yes, I thought, but we are the ones who will be left.

Once again, I was hearing, don't feel, just keep it all inside. I was at a breaking point.

It took two long months for surgery and the results. No one ever told us that it could have been a mistake. The day we went to the oncologist's office for the final results, I stayed in the waiting room. I couldn't bear to hear the words, it's terminal. My daughter had flown in from British Columbia, to be with Autumn before we received the results. When they came out of the doctor's office there were no tears, and the doctor called me in. He delivered news we didn't expect to hear.

"It's not malignant."

We all hugged him and then one another. I felt a pang of guilt walking past both the cancer survivors, and those who didn't stand a chance, as we left Princess Margaret Hospital in downtown Toronto.

Autumn and I have become the comfort of old shoes, questions we can't answer, and answers we may be reluctant to give. We remember where we started and thought we could go, our shoes still line up on a common mat. At the beginning, we sat at the water's edge and talked about a future too far in the distance to imagine. What we thought we wanted, is what we have now.

At the onset of Autumn's diagnosis, I found a therapist. The thought of losing my best friend was overwhelming. My childhood anxiety hadn't left me, it was embedded deep inside me. Memories from my childhood were beginning to surface, largely around the death of my six-year-old brother, Patrick. I had kept my childhood trauma to myself. With my therapist Jane, I found someone I trusted and allowed myself to revisit my old tapes.

My mother's early penchant for disastrous thoughts, was an old tape still replaying in my head. I began to think about some of her early admissions to me. These were common repeated phrases.

"You would stand in your crib and shake when you heard his voice."

Then the one often repeated that struck fear in me as a young child.

"Don't worry about next week, we could all be dead by then."

Feeling anything in my family wasn't acceptable. No one talked about their feelings. It was a house of secrets. I began to search for a solution with my mother from the age of four.

Trauma was deeply rooted in me. I was always ready to run.

With Jane I began to unravel my childhood experience. She was surprised that I was the survivor I appeared to be. Outwardly that was true, but there were health repercussions. My poor cardiovascular health was one indicator of the stress I'd lived with all those years. As Jane delved into my childhood, it was clear there were no firm attachments. I grew up in fear of my father until I left home at fourteen. There was no sense of safety anywhere. I loved my mother and when she wasn't working from dawn to dusk, she was there for us. She didn't have a place of safety, so how could she give one to me? My body carried the memory of the fear I lived with. I reacted and jumped at loud noises. I couldn't tolerate angry voices, or even loud debates.

Living with uncertainty had become my normal. Was I deserving? Rejection was difficult to handle. It would take decades before I felt I could fit somewhere. The roots of my fear ran deep, my body memory strong, I was rejected before I was born. Jane and I tore up the old tapes one by one. My anxiety was replaced with positive affirmations about how far I'd come, and where I could go. Jane and I changed my life. Our six-year therapeutic relationship gave me the courage to regain some of the confidence I had as a teenager. There are still remnants of my mother's version of waiting for the sky to fall, but now I understand the reasons. I know it's never too late. In my seventies, I knew that life was a series of connected events. In my youth I waited for a defining moment when I would wake up one day to a revelation.

"This is it, this is the moment you've been waiting for, where it all makes sense."

It never happened. As moments fell into days, and months into years, those moments and events gradually morphed into a chain of memories. There was a new awakening around relationships and love as I grew older. Everything I knew was based on the traditional values I had grown up with. As a late teen, I had thoughts about finding my way to a Kibbutz in Israel, or Findhorn, in Scotland. I gravitated towards living in community.

I love people, and I love the feeling that loving people gives me. Diversity in relationships became more apparent when I moved back to Toronto. When I was looking for a cinematographer for my first short film, I met Davina Hader. Davina is one of the most beautiful, gentle women I have ever known. Davina and I made my first short film together the year I turned seventy-one. We were welcomed into several festivals in the United States and our film, "Hushed," won a Best Female film award at, The Virgin Springs Cinefest in Kolkata, India. Later we were invited to attend an international red-carpet event. I felt a new energy and drive to create as I aged. Within a span of four years, I made a short film, saw three of my plays staged at, 'The Alumnae Theatre,' in Toronto at Gay Play Day, and wrote four features for Toronto's Pink Play magazine, about life stages. Some of my poetry, from my writer's trip to Ireland, was in an anthology.

The diversity I encountered later in life, made me look at gender and sexuality in a new way. Nothing was as cut and dried as old social norms made it out to be. I met women amid transition who had breasts, and a penis. I had friends who transitioned from male to female, and female to male. Some were denied access to their children, dismissed by their employers.

One of my best late life surprises was the affection and love that developed between me and an aging male rocker. I think our narrow definition of love, often prevents us from having loving relationships with people we meet along the way. Loving in a nonsexual way, denotes a love free of barriers and expectations. I have been fortunate to experience this level of a loving friendship numerous times in my life. I met one of them at the edge of Lake Ontario, on a mild summer evening. We were at a musical event at a local Marina. I moved away from the crowd to avoid cigarette smoke. He was meandering at the edge of the crowd, looking like a lost child.

"Do you mind if I join you?"

Standing in front of me was Pentti Glan. He had a tilt in his walk I would come to know. He was holding a cigarette.

"If you get rid of that, yes."

Pentti and I developed a close bond in a short period of time. He would call me just to tell me how much he loved me. His wonderful partner Karen joked, I'm just happy he's in love with a lesbian this time. Years before I might have rejected this unusual connection, but my definition of love had expanded. Pentti and I were the same age. We discussed our pasts, and our much shorter futures. We met for lunches, talked easily about life and simple things. He told me how his love of boats began. Bette Midler bought him his first boat to live on while they were filming, 'The Rose.' He played Bette's drummer in the film.

Pentti was very humble about his past, touring with Alice Cooper, Lou Reed, Three Dog Night, among others. I only saw the fan side of Pentti when my friend brought Paul Justman to our boat. Paul had produced and directed, "Standing in The Shadows of Motown," with our friend Mary as a co-producer. Pentti was adamant he wanted a picture with Paul. His partner Karen told us, after Pentti passed away.

"The photograph with Paul was one of his most loved possessions, and proudly displayed in a frame on the mantel."

I saw Pentti as a quaint sweet man, and I loved him dearly. He had so many moments that were endearing. I can still see him gliding like an awkward ballet dancer, unsure of his next step. His head was usually tilted to one side when he spoke, his voice soft. He was the embodiment of authenticity. The year before he left us, I had a birthday cake made for him with the inscription,

"The Beat goes On."

Somewhere in a place that we hope exists, his beat will go on. The rhythm of life, our memories and the love we can carry in our hearts.

*Autumn's Aunty Olga standing in front of their store
on Queen Street, Toronto, Ontario.*

*Megan and Davina Hader on the Merry
Go Round at Port Dalhousie Park,
Ontario.*

*Jean and Liz - friends in British Columbia
who testified at Megan's trial for her
motorhome accident.*

Madison Morrison
(Granddaughter) and
Tolstoy's Grandson at
the Doukhobor's 100th
Anniversary of Arriving
in Canada.

Megan and Autumn in
Kingston, Ontario.

Pentti Glan and Megan

75 and very alive - at Waverly Park in Fort Erie, Ontario.

*Syl in her 70's and
Megan*

CHAPTER TWENTY

The Letters

The year before my mother left us, her life unraveled with a phone call from a stranger. I could only imagine what that looked like for her. On the other side of the country, the letters she'd written to her long-lost love had been found in an attic. She was finishing her small supper and had just tuned into, 'The Price is Right,' when the phone rang. She stood up slowly shuffling over to grab the phone on the third ring.

"Yes, yes, this is her, who did you say you are?"

"You found what?"

Her mind was racing. Her secret past, folded into yellow pages, her red lipstick kisses still visible. The promise of a forever that never came. She fumbled under the phone table for her can of Vogue tobacco, her arthritic hands shaking, while she cradled the receiver on her left shoulder. She removed the loose tobacco and slid it with quick precision onto the thin white paper. Taking a long drag from her cigarette, a piece of hot ash fell to the floor.

"In whose attic?"

She smudged the ash out with her slipper. The stranger continued.

"My father passed away, and we were cleaning out his house, we found letters and pictures in a box in his attic, they are of you and our father, with a small boy."

She wondered how he found her.

"I tracked you down and found your son."

My mother was almost speechless. Although she'd long given up hope they'd be reunited, now she had confirmation there would never be a chance to see Hugh again. After the conversation ended, she made her way to the window. She rolled another cigarette and stood for a long time staring out into the dark night.

My mother carefully removed the small photograph from her wallet, repeating what had been a constant, quiet ritual over the past six decades. She drew it to her lips and pressed it into her wet cheek. It was faded, and small pieces were missing, just like her memories. A dark-haired woman and a handsome man in a World War Two uniform stood together, obviously in love. This was who she was, before unseen circumstances turned her life in a direction she could never have imagined. The war didn't just leave casualties in the trenches. It reached out, interrupted lives and ran roughshod over dreams. She slid the photograph carefully back into her wallet, and watched the snow begin to accumulate on the giant fir tree until it became a thick white blur. Now it was just a matter of waiting for the package of letters to arrive in the mail. Syl wondered if the question she had for decades, would be answered.

"Why didn't you come back for us like you promised?"

She took solace in knowing that he'd never forgotten her, that he had preserved her letters all these years. Her last letter to him arrived along with all the others.

Dear Hugh: December 6, 1945:

    I don't understand why you stopped writing to me. You know I am waiting for you to come back. It was a mistake to trust that John would keep his word. He's a mean-spirited Goddamn liar. I'm going to find a way out of this. Do you remember daddy saying he'd find me a lawyer? He sees it too, and so do my brothers. I'm not expecting his child, that's a lie too.

Please write back soon, I love you and know you love me.

All our love, Syl, and Sonny.

    No letter came. She knew she was about four months pregnant with John's child. Syl continued her attempts to abort. Her lipstick kisses from decades past, a reminder of her once full lips, the lines still vibrant. The last letter in the package was not from her, it was from John.

It answered a lifetime of questions.

Dear Hugh: November 1945.

I know you are home now and probably thinking about contacting Syl. I found all the letters you wrote to her during the war. I burned them. She is my legal wife, and I don't plan to let her go. She's expecting my child. Do us all a favour and forget about her. I hope you'll do the right thing. Yours truly,

John.

I would unknowingly become part of my mother's past, clinging to life inside a hostile womb, born into a war zone that would be my childhood. I knew very early in my life I could survive almost anything and in the end my mother had gifted me with a tenacious spirit. Looking back at my life there isn't anything I would change.

The inscription I put on her headstone revealed my last wish for her.

"Asleep in the arms of an angel."

I could only hope it was true.

About the Author

Free spirit. Born in the Selkirk Mountains. Roamed for the first three years with bears, moose and deer. Mother's constant warning, "When you're out playing, watch out for the Grizzly bears."

Gradually Megan integrated into a world void of wildlife. At an early age, she began to store her feelings in poetry and stories in a box under her bed.

Along the way, she dabbled in theatre, got a degree in Social Work, worked in Alberta with abused women on the Blood Reserve and tried to make a difference. She woke up recently and was shocked she was entering her 7th decade. The boxes under her bed had multiplied. Some of it had found its way to anthologies, magazines, and the stage, but the boxes were full of half a century of a life filled with stories yet to be told.

During her teenage years, Megan often spent time alone at English Bay in Vancouver, sitting on her 'writing rock' with pen and paper in hand. As a young adult in the 1960s, she read her poetry at coffee houses such as The Bunkhouse and Sequel alongside other visiting artists like Sonny Terry, Brownie McGhee, Jose Feliciano, and David Whiffen. These gatherings provided a respite for those seeking relief from the Vietnam War. Megan has been writing since she was seven years old.

https://brainspiredpublishing.com/megan-hutton

Printed in the USA
CPSIA information can be obtained
at www.ICGtesting.com
LVHW031215110124
768681LV00043B/383